ENUMA ELISH

The Babylonian Creation Epic

*also includes 'Atrahasis',
the first Great Flood myth*

TIMOTHY J. STEPHANY

ISBN-13: 978-1493775033
ISBN-10: 1493775030

Printed in the United States of America by Createspace

http://www.timothyjstephany.com

Contents

other books by TIMOTHY J. STEPHANY

Introduction

The Babylonian Creation story, known in ancient times by its opening words 'Enuma Elish' (meaning 'when the heavens above') is a concise presentation of Mesopotamian lore concerning the origins of the gods, the universe, and mankind. Although it is not certain just how far back the fundamental conceptions of this creation were first comprehended, they no doubt far precede this particular version of the Babylonian Creation, which was uncovered as tablets from the ancient city of Nineveh dating to the 7th century BC. Yet these tablets hold within them a composition which may have arisen towards the close of the 2nd millennium BC, made up of earlier material dating from the Bronze Age.

Apart from its age and provenance, what is of interest in considering this creation myth and other Mesopotamian myths is the same which holds for any story that deals with essential human concerns—which have remained unchanged through time and history. Thus such myths, dealing with the origins of humanity, also emphasize basic human preoccupations; acting as a means to explain the origin of our collective existence. Likewise, they stretch back as far as we are capable of reaching in reviewing the earliest written works of humanity; and containing beliefs, concerns, and the manner of life of men in the early phases of civilization. Likewise, their importance ranges wide based upon how far such seminal myths were shared among humanity, with characters who infuse world mythology, and which are still known to us today, even if under different names.[*] Thus while the characters of Apsu, Tiamat, and Marduk are not widely familiar in the modern world, some of these have found their way via other Near Eastern myths to become known to us, specifically through the pages of the Bible.

Most conspicuous among these is the name of Marduk, the great Babylonian sky god, who appears in the book of *Esther* as Mordecai the Benjaminite—as also does the goddess Ishtar appear as Esther herself. The deity Apsu represents the watery abyss which was believed, since before the Classical Age, to underlie the earth; and this conception holds in references to the Abyss. But the name of Tiamat is also retained within the *Genesis* chapter 1 word for the 'deep', which is '*tehom*'; also used in the book of *Isaiah*.[1]

> *Awake, awake, put on strength, O arm of the LORD; awake, as in the ancient days, in the generations of old. Art thou not it that hath cut Rahab, and wounded the dragon? Art thou not it which hath dried the sea, the waters of the great deep [tehom]; that hath made the depths of the sea a way for the ransomed to pass over?* **(Isaiah 51:9-10, KJV)**

---

[*] See *Blood & Incest* and *The Eden Enigma: A Dialogue*

And it is Isaiah who also forecasts the future display of Yahweh's might, recalling the deeds of his past, in saying:

> In that day the LORD with his sore and great and strong sword shall punish leviathan the piercing serpent, even leviathan that crooked serpent; and he shall slay the dragon that is in the sea. (**Isaiah 27:1, KJV**)

Thus in this sense the two gods of the fresh-water and salt-water, Apsu and Tiamat, might be most easily identified with the male and female Leviathans.* And this primordial deep, at first enshrouded in darkness, also acts as the cauldron from which the creation of *Genesis* takes place. This cosmic sea was then populated by Leviathan and a number of other denizens from which the world was fashioned by God, just as it is with Marduk's creation found in 'Enuma Elish':

> Thou didst divide the sea by thy strength: thou brakest the heads of the dragons in the waters. Thou brakest the heads of leviathan in pieces, and gavest him to be meat to the people inhabiting the wilderness. (**Psalms 74:13-14, KJV**)

The conflict between the sky god and primordial serpent is often viewed in myth as being perpetual between the two, as long as the world endures; illustrated in the battle between Thor and the Midgard Serpent or Krishna and the dragon, Kalli Naga[†]:

> Thou rulest the raging of the sea: when the waves thereof arise, thou stillest them. Thou hast broken Rahab in pieces, as one that is slain; thou hast scattered thine enemies with thy strong arm. The heavens are thine, the earth also is thine: as for the world and the fulness thereof, thou hast founded them. (**Psalms 89:9-11, KJV**)

This likewise is related to God setting the boundary of the sea, which is mentioned in the Apocryphal *Prayer of Manasseh* (2-3). In other words, God assured that the sea was not allowed to exceed its limits, which would otherwise obliterate life on land.

This correspondence between 'Enuma Elish' and the Biblical creation, however, goes far deeper, in the recognition that the very order of the creation of *Genesis* chapter 1 is reflected in the generations of gods in 'Enuma Elish', which is enumerated in the following table:

---

* The female Leviathan was killed and pickled, while the male Leviathan will be attacked by angels in the final days before Leviathan and Behemoth engage in a contest which claims both their lives. ('Haggadah'; see Barnstone 1984: 22) The role of providing food for the righteous is also taken by Leviathan and Behemoth.

[†] See *Roar of the Tempests: A Dialogue*

Genesis Creation	Generation of gods	God of
Day 1 – light from dark[*]	3 – Anshar and Kishar	the two semi-spheres
Day 2 – water separation	1 – Apsu and Tiamat	the fresh and salt water
Day 3 – dry land	2 – Lahmu and Lahamu	the silt-lands
Day 4 – heavens made	4 – Anu	the heavens
Day 5 – oceans made	5 – Ea (Nudimmud)	the waters
Day 6 – mankind made	6 – Marduk	(creator of mankind)
Day 7 – God rests	(gods relieved from labors)	

Correspondences between Genesis creation and Enuma Elish creation[2]

And here, just as Yahweh in resting upon the seventh day establishes henceforth the holiness of that day, the Sabbath Day, so too in 'Enuma Elish' is the creation of man followed by their construction of a temple called Esagila (Tablet 6); *likewise*, with the establishment of religious rituals, sacrifices, and practices; and even the seven ranks of cultic initiation.

This underscores the importance of 'Enuma Elish' at the mythological level, but on the level of paleoastronomy, or searching out stellar knowledge, the creation myth associates the defeat of Apsu and Tiamat with the establishment of cosmic forces as designated in Tablet 5; which is like the forces of order overcoming the forces of chaos, even as a personified Chaos. However, the most useful section in this regard is lacking, due to breaks in the tablet itself, and thus it has been 'restored' through the utilization of information from astrological tablets—which are plentiful, however—to simulate what these missing verses might have been like. But the end result remains yet unsatisfying, because the meaningfulness of the passages is lost even if its content and style might be mimicked in the cause of reconstructing the complete tale. But preceding this gap there is enough to provide some basic information about their calendar: of a 12-month year with each month being 30 days, and this is made clear through its definition of the character of the moon, as it waxes and wanes through the month.

Beyond this the Babylonian creation epic proceeds to its inevitable conclusion, with the conflict of cosmic forces leading to the eventual creation of the world and of mankind. And this latter is itself taken up in the myth following, 'Atrahasis', which is one which runs similarly to the Noah story of *Genesis*. But while the name of Noah and some of the tale's other details arise from Apamea in Phrygia,[3] the survivor of the Great Flood in the

---

[*] Yahweh performs his creation by daylight: "And then was the spirit, and darkness and silence were on every side; the sound of man's voice was not yet formed. Then commandedst thou a fair light to come forth of thy treasures, that thy work might appear." (II Esdras 6:39-40)

original Hebrew version appears to have been rather the patriarch Abraham!* This is both apparent from the similarity between their two names (Atrahasis/Abraham), but likewise the words which God speaks to Abraham, as the only remaining segment to be retained, are not unique among other world flood myths:

> *And the LORD said unto Abram…Lift up now thine eyes, and look from the place where thou art northward, and southward, and eastward, and westward: For all the land which thou seest, to thee will I give it, and to thy seed for ever. And I will make thy seed as the dust of the earth: so that if a man can number the dust of the earth, then shall thy seed also be numbered. Arise, walk through the land in the length of it and in the breadth of it; for I will give it unto thee. (**Genesis 13:14-17, KJV**)*

Here the god tells the lone survivor of the flood that the earth he sees stretching out around him henceforth belongs to himself and all of his descendants; given that beasts and giants of the prior age (evidenced by the bones of Mesozoic reptiles and Pleistocene mega-fauna) have all been wiped out. This has been transmogrified completely by the Biblical editors into the conferring of the land of Canaan unto Abraham and his descendants through Isaac and Jacob, which served a more immediate political purpose at a far later time.

Yet there remained the trouble mankind caused for the gods, which arose from his incessant noise, exponential increase, and unlimited lifespan. Thus the gods must take steps to assure that man does not come to grow so numerous yet again, and thus the gods bring mortality to mankind, along with a range of other plagues to beset him. And thus is the stage set for the following history of mankind.

> *And the LORD said, My spirit shall not always strive with man, for that he also is flesh: yet his days shall be an hundred and twenty years. (**Genesis 6:3, KJV**)*

Although the gods are at the same time convinced that humankind must never come to an end, due to the delight they enjoy from the sacrifices made to them. And this is even included in the conclusion of the Noah flood, where he makes his sacrifices, a pleasing odor to God, which causes him to pledge that he will never destroy the entire earth again:

> *And Noah builded an altar unto the LORD; and took of every clean beast, and of every clean fowl, and offered burnt offerings on the altar. And the LORD smelled a sweet savour; and the LORD said in his heart, I will not again curse the ground any more for man's sake; for the imagination of man's heart is evil from his youth; neither will I again smite any more every thing living, as I have done. While the*

---

* See *Roar of the Tempests: A Dialogue* and *Blood & Incest*

*earth remaineth, seedtime and harvest, and cold and heat, and summer and winter, and day and night shall not cease. (**Genesis 8:20-22, KJV**)*

He subsequently leaves his bow (rainbow) as an indicator of this, symbolic of the covenant made with mankind; just as in 'Enuma Elish' the bow Marduk uses to slay Tiamat, to still the raging sea, is hung up in the heavens as the 'Bow Star' (*Canis Major*) by the sky god Anu. Then in the case of 'Atrahasis' the rainbow is depicted rather as the necklace of Nintu/Belet-ili. And the rainbow is commonly held to be the necklace of the mother goddess;[4] as in the case of the retrieval of the Norse goddess Freyia's necklace after a battle is fought between its thief (Loki) and its rescuer (Heimdall), the gods of fire and water, in the form of a cloudburst. Yet it must also be that the Mother Goddess was known to wear an actual necklace made in the shape of flies, which were apparently created by Anu and were henceforth to decorate her chest in eternal memory of the Great Flood. Thus there appears to be some intermingling of conceptions, as here the necklace which appears is one no doubt familiar and particular to Nintu, rather than the goddess setting forth the rainbow as an eternal reminder of the flood; associated with her own covenant with mankind, which she makes clear when she declares, "He must now save me from any harm, by offering sacrifice."

Although it is not likely that the 'Book of Genesis' stories of the creation and flood were immediately aware of or based upon these original Mesopotamian myths, they certainly would have been inheritors of the various mythological traditions of the Near East when the Biblical books were in the process of being composed during the 6th through 2nd centuries BC.[*] But these episodes are not important merely from their having close Biblical parallels, rather it is beneficial to view them within the very same context of theological conceptions and comprehensions of any other period of time, since these verses once served the very purpose of providing explanations for the ways of the world and the experiences of man. This theological and sociological significance can be seen in how the poem 'Enuma Elish' was utilized annually at the New Year's festival at Babylon, where it would be openly recited or even acted out; as a symbolic recurrence of the creation coincident with the 'creation' of the new year.

And it is known that the semi-historical work of Berossus (*Babyloniaca*) is a product of Hellenistic times, which is precisely the period when the so-called 'Priestly' ('P') document was being composed or brought together. This is recognizable in the correspondence between Berossus' 432,000 years given for the rule of the ten antediluvian kings, which in *Genesis* is given as a duration of 1,656 years. But 432,000 years is 86,400 x 5, while 1,656 years is 86,400 weeks, and thus there remains a clear uniformity between them.[5] But this does not insist that the writers of 'P' were aware of Berossus' work—though they may have been—only that they would have had access to some of the very materials which were knocking about the Near East during that

---

[*] See *The Holy Bible Revealed, Volume 2: Compositional History*

antiquarian age. For instance, in the Biblical flood story the chief character is named Noah, while in Berossus it is Ziusudra who is the Sumerian character. And the name of this Ziusudra is related to that of Atrahasis through his epithet 'the faraway' ('*sudra*').[6] While the name Utnapishtim also appears to be related to Noah through the syllable '*nah*'. Likewise, there exist parallels with the releasing of a dove and a raven, as well as the boat coming to rest upon a mountain top (provided from the 'Gilgamesh Cycle'), although the detail of the olive branch would have arisen from Palestine rather than Mesopotamia.[7]

The received form of 'Atrahasis' is also older than that of 'Enuma Elish', and dated to around 1700 BC, thus it also precedes its Biblical doppelganger by at least 1,000 years. Likewise, the story of Atrahasis surely held a prominent place in Bronze Age Mesopotamia—if we can permit ourselves for a moment to imagine an Earth prior to the period of Biblical prominence—from its similar emphasis upon both the creation and plight of man; so that it was even included as an episode within the 'Gilgamesh Cycle'. In this story the man who survived the flood, Utnapishtim, was the only one to have gained or retained his immortality.[*] Yet there is a sweeping connection between these formative events of the world, as performed by the gods, and conceptions of eternity and immortality, which established the firm distinction between the realm of heaven and that of earth. Though it is still made clear in the creation story that humanity is a product of the divine, and must be reminded that although his body is mortal that his spirit is immortal (Tablet 1).

Taken together, these two stories ought to be viewed in the same manner that any ancient myths ought to be, downplaying the necessity for a unified and continuous narrative as the Holy Bible follows, since it must be viewed that these Biblical myths too once existed in this same form as did their Babylonian counterparts before they were collected and assembled together as we have inherited them in the Biblical canon. Yet the same thing could have been done with these Babylonian myths, or indeed any mythological tradition, if the right dynamics and motives had coincided at a particularly propitious moment, as it did among the Hebrews beginning in the 6th century BC. Yet given their force, starkness, and even archetypical familiarity, these Mesopotamian myths can still be given the breath of life anew, and serve a purpose greater than that of mere historical value, but rather to be taken as works of imaginative literature to be considered, felt, and enjoyed.

---

[*] See *The Gilgamesh Cycle*

ENUMA ELISH

TABLET 1

At a time when even the glories above had yet to be named,[*]

And unuttered was the word for the world which lay beneath

It was then that the first being, Apsu, who was their source,

And the progenitor Tiamat, the mother who gave birth to all,

Intermingled their waters, producing neither field nor marsh

At a time when no divine beings had yet come into existence,

There were no names to be spoken, and no fates pronounced,

But the gods were given birth within those intermixing waves

The first were Lahmu and Lahamu,[†] their names were spoken

But once they had fully grown and become mature of form,

Then were born Anshar and Kishar, and they outshone them

And so many days passed by, and many years were counted

Their first son was Anu, being as great as any of his forebears

And Anshar caused his son Anu to become just like himself

From Anu came Nudimmud, who was also his spitting image

And Nudimmud proved to be even greater than his forebears[‡]

Profoundly wise and full of insight, with strength in his limbs

More infused with might than even his grandfather Anshar

---

[*] Compare with II Esdras 6:4 – 'before the measures of the firmament were named'

[†] These are Ea and Damkina according to the Assyrian version (Dalley 2000: 274). The word *lahmu* means 'muddy', usually describing the men who inhabit the watery abyss, the Apsu.

[‡] This is the god Ea, also known as Enki, lord of the Apsu

With none among the gods who could be considered his equal
That generation of gods would gather together for wild revels
So they proved bothersome to Tiamat, their hullabaloo echoed
All this commotion proved unsettling to Tiamat's inner being,
And she was bothered by all of their activity within Anduruna[*]
There was nothing Apsu could do to mitigate their carousing
But there was nothing Tiamat would say to quiet them down,
And no matter how troublesome their conduct became to her,
Regardless of how rowdy things were, she just put up with it
This kept up until divine Apsu, the source of the mighty gods,
Summoned to him and spoke to his officer Mummu, saying,
"Hear me Mummu, my trusted officer who I can rely upon,
Come with me, and together we will go to speak with Tiamat!"
Thus they went together and seated themselves before Tiamat,
And they conversed with her about their children, the gods,
Apsu raised his voice to be heard, speaking heartily to Tiamat,
"I have been very troubled by the manner of their conduct,
So that I cannot relax during the day, nor sleep well at night
Therefore I shall bring it to a halt, and get rid of them all!
Then silence shall reign, and thus we might get some sleep."
But as soon as Tiamat heard his words she became incensed,
Overcome with ire, she screamed intensely at her husband,
But then she soothed the fury that raged within her breast,

---

[*] A dwelling place of the gods

"Could we permit our own offspring to be thus eradicated?

Despite their troublesome ways, we ought to put up with it."

Then the officer Mummu provided his own answer to Apsu,

But he spoke at odds with the advice of his mother, the earth,

"Father, you ought to put an end to their annoying behavior,

That one might relax during the day and sleep well at night."

Apsu was in full agreement with what he said, and satisfied

With thoughts of devising a vile plan for his sons, the gods,

His officer Mummu put his arms around him, hugging him,

And fell down at his knees and enthusiastically kissed him

Yet what they planned was conveyed to their sons, the gods,

For they heard everything and were troubled, pacing about,

They all grew quite quiet, and sat around without speaking

Until the god with the gift for wisdom and understanding,

Ea, the god who is insightful, recognized their intentions,

And he formulated a solution for it all, planning it out well

He concocted it with superlative skill, his spell was perfect,

For when he chanted it, he calmed the turbulent waters

And abounding sleep overcame Apsu; he became pacified

He caused him to enter a deep sleep, seeped in tranquility

While the officer Mummu, his advisor, was left in a trance

Then Ea removed his belt and took his crown from his head,

And took his Mantle of Brilliance and dressed himself in it

Then he forced Apsu down under his feet and crushed him

Enuma Elish

And bound Mummu, laying him down over him crosswise,[*]
Then he established his own residence on top of the Apsu,
And he then took Mummu, holding him by a nose-leash,
And after he had subdued and then killed all of his foes,
Then Ea raised a declaration of victory over his adversaries
Then he could rest easy within his own personal chambers
And these he named 'Apsu', and established temples there
Making it his home, Ea lived in luxury with his wife Damkina
There within the House of Fate, there in the Hall of Purpose

Then the Lord came, who among all was the most judicious,
There within the watery Apsu did Marduk take his shape,
Within the unsullied waters of the Apsu was Marduk born,
From his father Ea, his mother Damkina gave birth to him
He was suckled on the milk of the goddess's own breasts
And she who breastfed him embodied him with excellence,
So that he had a lofty stature; the look of his eyes was intense,
Mature from the very first, and mighty even at a young age

_____

[*] Compare with the Prayer of Manasseh 1:3 – "who hast bound the sea by the word of thy commandment; who hast shut up the deep, and sealed it by thy terrible and glorious name"; and Revelations 20:2-3 – "And he laid hold on the dragon, that old serpent, which is the Devil, and Satan, and bound him a thousand years, and cast him into the bottomless pit, and shut him up, and set a seal upon him, that he should deceive the nations no more, till the thousand years should be fulfilled: and after that he must be loosed a little season."

Tablet I

When his grandfather Anu looked upon him, he was glad,

His face shone greatly, his heart was exceedingly pleased,

So perfect that his head was twice as lofty as any other god

Rising high above them, he was the better by every measure

Both his arms and legs were well-formed beyond comparison

So that it could not be fathomed, almost incomprehensible,

Moreover he possessed four ears to hear and four eyes to see,

And red flames leapt forth whenever he opened his mouth,

His four ears were also considerable, of voluminous size,

As were his eyes, which were capable of perceiving anything

Being unsurpassed among the gods, of exceptional build,

Having limbs which were mighty, and a body terrifically tall

Then Anu cried, "Mariutu, my son, you are king of the gods!"[*]

Dressed in a shining robe fit for ten gods, rising beyond him,

There were five almighty beams which surmounted his head

And Anu invented the four winds and then fashioned them,

These he set in Marduk's hand, saying "Free them, my son!"

Then he formed dust and caused the tornado to bear it away,

Then he invented the tidal swell, which aggravated Tiamat

And Tiamat was agitated and unsettled both day and night

The gods,[*] meanwhile, were distressed and forced to endure,

---

[*] Mariutu ('son'), meaning Marduk

So with vile thoughts on their minds, they spoke to Tiamat,
"Because at the time that they killed your husband Apsu,
And you failed to stand by his side but rather sat by silently,
Thus did Anu invent the four strong winds and tidal swell,
So as to intentionally agitate you, so that we have no peace!
Did you not hold your husband Apsu within your heart?
And likewise the officer Mummu who was also captured?
It's not surprising you're forsaken! Are you not a mother?
You are unsettled both day and night, but look at our plight
Are we not distressed; have a heart, do you not care for us?
Look, we lack strength in our limbs, and our eyes are hollow
Free us from this distressing burden, that we might get sleep!
Raise the war cry; make them pay for what they have done!
Destroy this enemy; eradicate him entirely from off the earth!"
Tiamat listened to what they said, and she agreed with them,
"Yes, I think that we ought to do just as you have suggested,
The gods who dwell within the Apsu will suffer great misery,[†]
For they chose to do evil to those gods that gave them birth!"
And they gathered about and stood in proximity to Tiamat
They were brutal and planned endlessly both day and night
Grumbling and fuming, all done in the cause of making war

---

[*] Tiamat's demon brood, rather than the gods who dwell in heaven with Anu or the Apsu with Ea

[†] The gods who are with Ea

Tablet I

They called together a council of war to consider battle plans

Lady Hubur, who made all, produced an unfailing weapon,

She brought big snakes with piercing teeth and vicious fangs,

Their bodies she had infused with poison rather than blood

And she caused these raging dragons to emit deadly beams,

And to wear Mantles of Brilliance, so that they were like gods

(Then the Lady Hubur raised her voice, verbalizing the curse,)

"Anyone who gazes at them will be stricken down with horror!

They will always raise up their bodies and never back down!"

Then Tiamat enlisted a horned snake, a *mushussu*-dragon,

A *lahmu*-hero, an *ugallu*-devil, a mad dog, and scorpion-man,

Brutal *umu*-devils, a half-man half-fish, a half-man half-bull,

Carrying ruthless weaponry, and who reveal no fear in battle

Her commands were so portentous that none could be ignored

And in addition to these, she recruited eleven more likewise,

And above all of her children, of the gods who had assembled

She conferred upon Kingu the chief rank amongst them all,

Bestowing the generalship of her army and rule of the congress,

To hold aloft the spear to signify battle, to gather the warriors,

She had given him high command of the entire combat force,

And placed him to be seated upon the throne of rule, saying,

"I have conjured a spell in your name, making you foremost

Among the gods of congress! You now rule all of the gods!

You will reign supreme, for further you will be my sole mate!

Your orders shall not be disregarded amongst the Anukki!"

9

She conveyed to him the Tablet of Fate, clasping it at his chest,
"What you say will not be altered, and you will speak the law!"
So after Kingu had received his rank, been given Anu-power,
And had pronounced the fates of his sons, the gods, he said,
"What comes from out of your lips would obliterate flames!
Your potent poison would serve to incapacitate the mighty!"

TABLET II

Tiamat then called together the legions of her demon army

Assigning divisions to wage war against her sons, the gods

Tiamat caused more harm for future generations than Apsu

It was related to Ea that she was making war preparations

And Ea took heed of that communication upon receiving it

But he was left speechless and sat without uttering a word

After he considered it at length, however, his ire subsided,

He went to Anshar; stood before the one who fathered him,

And repeated to him everything relating to Tiamat's plans,

"O Father, Tiamat who gave all birth is set on destroying us!

She called together a congress and is like a deranged maniac

And the gods have all gone over to her side, every one of them

Even those which you gave rise to, have also joined her force

They have gathered around Tiamat and champion her cause

They were brutal and planned endlessly both day and night

Grumbling and fuming, all done in the cause of making war

They called together a council of war to consider battle plans

Lady Hubur, who made all, produced an unfailing weapon,

She brought big snakes with piercing teeth and vicious fangs,

Their bodies she had infused with poison rather than blood

And she caused these raging dragons to emit deadly beams,

And to wear Mantles of Brilliance, so that they were like gods

(Then the Lady Hubur raised her voice, verbalizing the curse,)

11

Enuma Elish

'Anyone who gazes at them will be stricken down with horror!
They will always raise up their bodies and never back down!'
Then Tiamat enlisted a horned snake, a *mushussu*-dragon,
A *lahmu*-hero, an *ugallu*-devil, a mad dog, and scorpion-man,
Brutal *umu*-devils, a half-man half-fish, a half-man half-bull,
Carrying ruthless weaponry, and who reveal no fear in battle
Her commands were so portentous that none could be ignored
And in addition to these, she recruited eleven more likewise,
And above all of her children, of the gods who had assembled,
She conferred upon Kingu the chief rank amongst them all,
Bestowing the generalship of her army and rule of the congress,
To hold aloft the spear to signify battle, and gather the warriors,
She had given him high command of the entire combat force,
And placed him to be seated upon the throne of rule, saying,
'I have conjured a spell in your name, making you foremost
Among the gods of congress! You now rule all of the gods!
You will reign supreme, for further you will be my sole mate!
Your orders shall not be disregarded among the Anukki!'
She conveyed to him the Tablet of Fate, clasping it at his chest,
'What you say will not be altered, and you will speak the law!'
So after Kingu had received his rank, been given Anu-power,
And had pronounced the fates of his sons, the gods, he said,
'What comes from out of your lips would obliterate flames!
Your potent poison would serve to incapacitate the mighty!'"

Anshar heard every word and found the news distressful,

"How awful!" were his first words, afterwards biting his lip,

And he was filled inside with anxiety, his muscles tightened

Yet the outburst at his son Ea proved anything but feeble,

"Son, you began this conflict, so you are responsible for it

For you went forth and killed Apsu, making Tiamat mad

Having done so, need we look any further for her enemy?"

The lord of prudence, source of wisdom, unsure what to do,

Nudimmud, with allaying words, replied well to Anshar,

"O my great father, incomprehensibly do you set destinies!

Holding in yourself the powers of creation and destruction!

O Anshar, incomprehensibly do you determine destinies!

Holding in yourself the powers of creation and destruction!

Please refrain from interrupting while I speak as I intend to

And keep in mind that my actions were right and justified

For before I killed Apsu, who was there for him to rely upon?

Whereas now there has emerged this assortment of demons

And before I could even approach and defeat him, Kingu,

He would already have annihilated me, and what then?"

Anshar heard every word and they were agreeable to him

And he was motivated thereby to speak to Ea, saying to him,

"Yes, son, your deeds were without doubt praiseworthy,

You can initiate your own attack, strong and determined

Ea, indeed your deeds were without doubt praiseworthy,

You can initiate your own attack, strong and determined

Go out and confront Tiamat, bring an end to her rebellion
May we pray only that her rage will subside from your spell."
And he heard the words spoken by his grandfather Anshar,
Then he went upon the roadway, veering neither right nor left
Ea continued on, keeping a lookout for Tiamat's battle-lines
But he did not make his voice heard, and instead returned
He went before Anshar, the king, and humbly beseeched him,
"Father, the ways of Tiamat are far too potent for me to handle
I went in search of her route, but my spell was inferior to hers
She holds powers that are alarming, and she is utterly horrific!
The forces about her are supreme, none could stand against her
Her great din never subsides, being too much for me to take
Her voice struck me with terror, so much that I headed back
Yet do not refrain, father, rather dispatch another against her
No matter how strong a woman, she still cannot equal a man
Thereby dispersing her legions, and confounding her orders;
This you must do before she overwhelms us with her powers."
Anshar spoke anxiously, addressing himself to his son Anu:
"My dependable son, who is as valiant as the *kasusu*-weapon,
Who possesses formidable power, and an unbearable charge,
Proceed to face Tiamat, and never fail to hold your position!
Cause her fury to withdraw and reduce her rage into stillness
But if she fails to listen, then beseech her so as to appease her."
And he heard every word that was spoken by his father Anshar,
Then he went upon the roadway, veering neither right nor left

Tablet II

Anu continued on, keeping a lookout for Tiamat's battle-lines
But he did not make his voice heard, and instead returned
He went before Anshar, the king, and humbly beseeched him,
"Father, the ways of Tiamat are far too potent for me to handle
I went in search of her route, but my spell was inferior to hers
She holds powers that are alarming, and she is utterly horrific!
The forces about her are supreme, none could stand against her
Her great din never subsides, being too much for me to take
Her voice struck me with terror, so much so that I headed back
Yet do not refrain, father, rather dispatch another against her
No matter how strong a woman, she still cannot equal a man
Thereby dispersing her legions, and confounding her orders;
This you must do before she overwhelms us with her powers."
Anshar could not find words, but cast his eyes unto the floor
He ground his teeth and could give no encouragement to Ea
So that all the Igigi gathered together, and all of the Anukki,
For a time they sat without speaking, lips closed, then spoke:
"Will not any god step forward, or is our fate predetermined?
Will not anyone go to confront Tiamat with **force of arms?**"*

Then from his secluded abode, Ea sent forth a declaration,

---

* Bold text is used throughout to indicate the restoration of a gap in the tablet due to damage;
if within brackets it is borrowed from within the same text; otherwise it is based upon
guesswork.

15

To the faultless one of Anshar, father of the mighty gods,
Him with a true heart, like a fellow citizen or countryman,
That formidable heir who was destined to defend his father,
Who strikes fearlessly into the fray, Marduk the Champion!
And he related to him the plans he had formulated, saying,
"Marduk, heed my counsel, give ear to your father's words,
The son of his who brings him confidence, go before Anshar,
Move in near to him, and make resolute declarations to him
All of his anxieties will take flight once you are before him."
And Lord Marduk was well pleased with his father's words,
Thus he went and approached, to stand in front of Anshar,
And Anshar gazed upon him, and his heart filled with glee
Then he kissed him upon the lips, and put aside his fears
(And Marduk raised his voice to be heard, saying to Anshar,)
"Father, you must not remain silent, but rather speak to me,
And permit me to go; let me do that which you wish me to do
Anshar, you must not remain silent, but rather speak to me,
And permit me to go; let me do that which you wish me to do."
(And Anshar raised his voice to be heard, saying to Marduk,)
"What sort of man would be willing to send you off to this war?
Son, this is Tiamat, a female, and she it is who will attack you."
(And Marduk raised his voice to be heard, saying to Anshar,)
"O Father, you brought me to life, be glad and of good cheer,
For soon your foot will be resting upon the very neck of Tiamat!
O Anshar, who brought me to life, be glad and of good cheer,

For soon your foot will be resting upon the very neck of Tiamat!"
(Then Anshar raised his voice to be heard, speaking to Marduk,)
"Go then, son, with my blessings, with all your superior wisdom!
And cut Tiamat down to size with your perfect incantations!
Go on your way at once, within the chariot of the storm-clouds
So that **her men** cannot advance, but rather make them retreat!"
And he was gladdened and spoke to his grandfather, saying,
"Ruler of the gods, deviser of the destinies of the high gods,
If I am to be your defender, and defeat Tiamat to preserve you,
Then assemble a commission, and proclaim a singular destiny,
And rest content among the others within Ubshu-ukkinakku*
For my own words rather than yours will determine destiny
Whatever I accomplish will not be undone, never overturned,
And the verdict that issues from my lips never be rescinded!"

---

* The hall of the divine congress

TABLET III

Then Anshar raised his voice to be heard, to his officer Kakka,

"Hear me Kakka, my trusted officer who I can depend upon,

I am sending you on a journey to go to Lahmu and Lahamu,

For you are good at ascertaining, a superlative communicator,

So that the gods, who are my fathers, will gather here to me

So that all of the gods will be assembled here in my presence

That we might then have a discussion; gather them for a feast

And give them plenty of bread to eat and the best of the wine

Then after have them declare a destiny for Marduk the Hero

So you must go soon, Kakka, and place yourself before them,

And convey to them everything that I will now relate to you:

Your son, Anshar, is the one who sent me to speak to you,

And he asked me to convey his own inner thoughts, saying,

Behold, Tiamat who gave all birth is determined to destroy us!

She called together a congress and is like a deranged maniac

And the gods have all gone over to her side, every one of them

Even those which you gave rise to have also joined her force

They have gathered around Tiamat and champion her cause

They were brutal and planned endlessly both day and night

Grumbling and fuming, all done in the cause of making war

They called together a council of war to consider battle plans

Lady Hubur, who made all, produced an unfailing weapon,

She brought big snakes with piercing teeth and vicious fangs,

18

Their bodies she had infused with poison rather than blood
And she caused these raging dragons to emit deadly beams,
And to wear Mantles of Brilliance, so that they were like gods
(Then the Lady Hubur raised her voice, verbalizing the curse,)
'Anyone who gazes at them will be stricken down with horror!
They will always raise up their bodies and never back down!'
Then Tiamat enlisted a horned snake, a *mushussu*-dragon,
A *lahmu*-hero, an *ugallu*-devil, a mad dog, and scorpion-man,
Brutal *umu*-devils, a half-man half-fish, a half-man half-bull,
Carrying ruthless weaponry, and who reveal no fear in battle
Her commands were so portentous that none could be ignored
And in addition to these, she recruited eleven more likewise,
And above all of her children, of the gods who had assembled,
She conferred upon Kingu the chief rank amongst them all,
Bestowing the generalship of her army and rule of the congress,
To hold aloft the spear to signify battle, and gather the warriors,
She had given him high command of the entire combat force,
And placed him to be seated upon the throne of rule, saying,
'I have conjured a spell in your name, making you foremost
Among the gods of congress! You now rule all of the gods!
You will reign supreme, for further you will be my sole mate!
Your orders shall not be disregarded among the Anukki!'
She conveyed to him the Tablet of Fate, clasping it at his chest,
'What you say will not be altered, and you will speak the law!'
So after Kingu had received his rank, been given Anu-power,

And had pronounced the fates of his sons, the gods, he said,
'What comes from out of your lips would obliterate flames!
Your potent poison would serve to incapacitate the mighty!'
So I sent forth Anu, but he was not able to stand up to her,
While Nudimmud was panic-stricken and merely came back
Until Marduk, your son, most capable of the gods, emerged
And he wished, of his own accord, to stand against Tiamat
He raised his voice to be heard, and spoke these words to me:
'If I am to be your defender, and defeat Tiamat to preserve you,
Then assemble a commission, and proclaim a singular destiny,
Then rest content among the others within Ubshu-ukkinakku
For my own words rather than yours will determine destiny
Whatever I accomplish will not be undone, never overturned,
And the verdict that issues from my lips never be rescinded!'
So act in haste, and declare a destiny for him with all speed,
That he might then go and confront your overwhelming foe!"

Thus Kakka went forth to carry out the mission given to him,
And in front of the gods Lahmu and Lahamu, his forebears,
He knelt down, kissing the ground which lay before them,
Then raised himself fully to stand, and related these words,
"Your son, Anshar, is the one who sent me to speak to you,
And he asked me to convey his own inner thoughts, saying,
Behold, Tiamat who gave all birth is determined to destroy us!
She called together a congress and is like a deranged maniac

Tablet III

And the gods have all gone over to her side, every one of them
Even those which you gave rise to have also joined her force,
They have gathered around Tiamat and champion her cause
They were brutal and planned endlessly both day and night
Grumbling and fuming, all done in the cause of making war
They called together a council of war to consider battle plans
Lady Hubur, who made all, produced an unfailing weapon,
She brought big snakes with piercing teeth and vicious fangs,
Their bodies she had infused with poison rather than blood
And she caused these raging dragons to emit deadly beams,
And to wear Mantles of Brilliance, so that they were like gods
(Then the Lady Hubur raised her voice, verbalizing the curse,)
'Anyone who gazes at them will be stricken down with horror!
They will always raise up their bodies and never back down!'
Then Tiamat enlisted a horned snake, a *mushussu*-dragon,
A *lahmu*-hero, an *ugallu*-devil, a mad dog, and scorpion-man,
Brutal *umu*-devils, a half-man half-fish, a half-man half-bull,
Carrying ruthless weaponry, and who reveal no fear in battle
Her commands were so portentous that none could be ignored
And in addition to these, she recruited eleven more likewise,
And above all of her children, of the gods who had assembled,
She conferred upon Kingu the chief rank amongst them all,
Bestowing the generalship of her army and rule of the congress,
To hold aloft the spear to signify battle, and gather the warriors,
She had given him high command of the entire combat force,

Enuma Elish

And placed him to be seated upon the throne of rule, saying,
'I have conjured a spell in your name, making you foremost
Among the gods of congress! You now rule all of the gods!
You will reign supreme, for further you will be my sole mate!
Your orders shall not be disregarded among the Anukki!'
She conveyed to him the Tablet of Fate, clasping it at his chest,
'What you say will not be altered, and you will speak the law!'
So after Kingu had received his rank, been given Anu-power,
And had pronounced the fates of his sons, the gods, he said,
'What comes from out of your lips would obliterate flames!
Your potent poison would serve to incapacitate the mighty!'
So I sent forth Anu, but he was not able to stand up to her
While Nudimmud was panic-stricken and merely came back
Until Marduk, your son, most capable of the gods, emerged
And he wished, of his own accord, to stand against Tiamat
He raised his voice to be heard, and spoke these words to me:
'If I am to be your defender, and defeat Tiamat to preserve you,
Then assemble a commission, and proclaim a singular destiny,
Then rest content among the others within Ubshu-ukkinakku
For my own words rather than yours will determine destiny
Whatever I accomplish will not be undone, never overturned,
And the verdict that issues from my lips never be rescinded!'
So act in haste, and declare a destiny for him with all speed,
That he might then go and confront your overwhelming foe!"

And Lahmu and Lahamu heard every word, and cried out,

And every one of the Igigi were overcome with sad moaning,

"But this is awful! For before Anshar sent us this intelligence,

We had not the least idea of what Tiamat was planning to do."

They made their way and gathered, the high gods who fix fate,

And they came into Anshar's company, being at once cheerful,

Greeting one another with kisses, and there in the meeting **hall**

They discussed among themselves, sitting together for a feast,

And they ate plenty of bread and imbibed the best of the wine

So that they slurped up flavorful beer through drinking straws

And were made full through the consumption of the alcohol

As a result of this they became cheerful, their hearts rejoiced,

And then they pronounced a destiny for Marduk their Hero.

TABLET IV

Then for his use they constructed for him a royal palace,
And he occupied it as ruler of his forebears, who declared,
"You, who are most revered among all of the high gods,
Your life is magnificent; your speech has the force of Anu!
Marduk, you are the most revered of any of the high gods,
Your life is magnificent; your speech has the force of Anu!
From henceforth your commands will never be distorted,
You hold the power to both raise up and to compel down,
Let your proclamations be law, and let your words be true
And not a single god will supersede the boundaries you set
Let there be an account created in support of your estate,
Like those required for the gods' temples, where they stand
You Marduk are our defender! You, lord, are our defender!
We must bestow upon you rule over the entire cosmic order
When seated in the council your words are second to none!
Let it be that your weapons never stray from their targets,
But rather let it be that your weapons crush your enemies!
Lord, be merciful towards the one who puts his faith in you
But also diminish the life of any god who is a worker of evil!"
Then they placed amongst themselves a single constellation,
And raised their voices to be heard, to Marduk, their son,
"Lord, may your proclamations be miraculous to the gods!
Speak orders for both destruction and for renewal, Amen!

Tablet IV

So proclaim to it that the constellation may then disappear!
Proclaim to it yet again that the constellation be seen again!"
Upon speaking, at his utterance the constellation disappeared
Speaking again, at his utterance the constellation reappeared
When his forebears, the gods, observed the power of his words,
Then they cried out in jubilation, declaring, "Marduk is King!"
Then bestowed unto him the scepter, throne, and staff of rule
And into his hand an unbeatable weapon to destroy his enemy
Then they cheered, "March forth, and sever the life of Tiamat!
May the winds carry her blood here to declare good tidings!"
Then his forebears, the gods, pronounced the fate of the Lord
Encouraging him to embody ideals of measure and restraint

Marduk created a bow and this he fashioned to be his weapon
Then fletched the arrow with feathers, and set it onto the string
Raising aloft a mace that he held within his rigid right hand
Slinging the bow over his arm, setting the quiver at his side
With lightning before him, eternal flame burning within him
He also fashioned a net which he could use to encircle Tiamat
He mastered the four winds so that she might have no escape
South Wind, North Wind, East Wind, and West Wind he took
Gifts from his father Anu that were kept at hand with the net
He generated the terror-gust, the tempest, and the whirlwind
Four gales and seven winds, the tornado and the hurricane
Setting forth the seven he had made, they followed behind

The Lord raised his mighty mace called the Flood-weapon
Before mounting his awesome, fear-rearing storm chariot
Harnessed to it was a quartet that had been strapped to it:
One called Killer, another Merciless, also Fleet and High-flyer
And their jaws were lowered, their teeth filled with venom,
They knew nothing of giving up, they knew only of attack
To the right of him he positioned both Blitzkrieg and Clasher,
And on the left he put another named Total Extermination!
Then dressed in a drapery of the most formidable armoring,
Upon his head was a halo blazing forth with a blinding glow
So the Lord thus set forth and travelled upon the roadway,
Heading in the direction of Tiamat, who rampaged wildly
Upon his tongue he held a spell, an incantation on his lips,
Holding within his hand a herb for protection against toxins
They all gathered about him, the gods amassed around him,
His forebears, gathered about him, they amassed around him
Then the Lord came near, setting his sights on Tiamat's heart
And attempted to divine the stratagem of Kingu, her partner
But as Kingu gazed out at him, his mind became bewildered
And his fortitude fell to pieces, his actions became awkward
As for his allies, the gods, those who had gone along with him,
When looking at this chief, the contender, they grew anxious
But Tiamat worked her magic, with no need to avert her gaze
Within her mouth there resided lies, deception, and cunning,
"Just how strong is this army you have with you, lord of gods?

The whole collection of them holds near to your own location!"
But the Lord held up his fearsome weapon, the Flood-weapon,
Conveying his words to Tiamat, who feigned kindness, saying,
"For what reason do you display this superficial benevolence,
When in your heart of hearts you generated a force for war?
Only because your sons, the gods, were making such a noise
Only because they have been inconsiderate of their forebears
But why ought you, who gave them birth, not forgive them?
You chose Kingu to be your partner, and also your war leader,
Bestowing unto him the Anu-power which he does not deserve,
And acted in enmity towards Anshar, honored king of gods
Thus you have multiplied the evils done against my forebears!
So make your army ready, equipped with what arms you have!
Or step forward yourself, that we might engage one on one!"
As soon as Tiamat had heard this speech that he had given,
She went ballistic, and flew into a wild and unstoppable rage,
With no little emotion, Tiamat bawled at the top of her lungs
And her viscera trembled all together to her very foundation
Undeterred in discharging her magic, she then spoke spells
At the same time, the warriors were busy honing their blades
Tiamat and Marduk, defender of the gods, faced one another
Moving towards each other, preparing for the coming clash
The Lord unleashed his net, and cast it out to entrap Tiamat
He called from behind him the terror-gust to fly in her face
Tiamat figured to open her mouth so as to swallow the wind

Enuma Elish

But the great force of the terror-gust kept her mouth open
The raging winds bloated her belly, she spread her jaws wide
Marduk released an arrow which struck her distended middle
Then he cleaved her into two pieces and cut open her heart,
Having defeated her, thus bringing her hateful life to an end
Tossing her down onto the dirt and setting his feet upon her
And after this, when he had killed their war leader, Tiamat,
He caused their legions to disperse, her army was in disarray
And the gods who were her allies, who had stood beside her,
All of them shook in fear, were struck with terror, and fled
Yet he allowed them to give themselves up, sparing them,
Since they were at once encircled, and not allowed to escape
So he had them bound and destroyed all of their weaponry
And they were trapped within a net and there they remained
Then they shrank back, overcome as they were by despair
But they endured this affliction, of being held incarcerated,
And concerning the several demons emitting deadly beams,
These being the army of creatures who passed to her right,
He attached onto them nose-leashes and bound their limbs
Then he crushed underfoot their foul instruments of warfare
Regarding Kingu, who was the highest ranked among them,
He ruined him, adding him to the tally of the other defeated,
Seizing from him the Tablet of Fate, which he did not deserve,
And impressed upon it his own seal, clasping it at his chest
Then after he had overcome and destroyed his adversaries,

Tablet IV

Announcing that the defeated enemy were now his slaves,
He provoked a song of victory of Anshar over all of his foes,
Realizing the plans which were formulated by Nudimmud
The warrior Marduk now dominated the incarcerated gods

To Tiamat he now turned his attention, the one he had caught
And the Lord Marduk trod upon the lower parts of her body
Raising his merciless hammer high he pulverized her skull
Then sliced open the arteries that carried her watery blood
He caused the North Wind to take it, to convey good tidings
When his forebears saw it they were jubilant and all sang out,
Then made plans to meet him with presents, gifts of greeting
The Lord took a moment to rest and looked over her corpse
He split the monster's cadaver and made marvelous things
Severing it up the middle, flaying it in half like a drying fish
One of which he thrust up to make the vault of the heavens
He drew a gate in front of it, put into the care of a guardian
Her waters were bounded, so that they might not surge free
And he went forth traversing the sky, seeking a holy place,
He made the Apsu, Nudimmud's dwelling, entirely smooth,
And the Lord then measured out the Apsu's total dimensions
The immense shrine which he built to resemble it was Esharra,
And in the temple Esharra, which he made to resemble heaven,
There he placed the centers of veneration for Anu, Ellil, and Ea.

TABLET V

He constructed various stations for every one of the high gods
And concerning the stars, he placed constellations for each one
Then he established the year and set forth its subdivisions
He assigned three stars to signify each of the twelve months[*]
And as he formulated his intentions for every day of the year,
He set forth the station of Neberu to delineate their movement[†]
That not one of them would veer from its appointed course
In addition, he established the stations made for Ellil and Ea[‡]
And made passages which passed through the two rib-racks,
Likewise forming a hatch both to the left and to the right[§]
While her liver was placed so as to locate the highest point
He brought into existence the crescent moon to rule night
And he assigned this night-gem to be an indicator of days,
"Never fail from proceeding each month in a circle of light,
Upon the first of the month, spread your light to all lands
You arise bright with your horns, as an indicator of six days

---

[*] Known as 'three stars each'

[†] Neberu is the planet Jupiter

[‡] Probably the two hemispheres, for the stars of the northern hemisphere were those of Ellil and the stars of the southern hemisphere were those of Ea, while the equatorial ones were those of Anu.

[§] That is, to the east and to the west

Tablet V

And upon the seventh day your crown is half in darkness [*]
The fifteenth day will be halfway, at every month's midpoint [†]
A time when Shamash faces you from the opposite horizon
Then slowly begin to diminish in appearance as you wane,
Make the day you are invisible near the track of Shamash, [‡]
Upon the thirtieth day, perform calibrations for the year, [§]
Because Shamash ultimately determines the year's length
Whenever there is an indicator, proceed over its own course
Then do not fail to enter the hall of judgement and decide:
Make your selection of the Bow Star for robbery and war, [8**]
Make your choice Ninmah for pregnancy and the unborn,
Make your choice the Harrow for the fertility of the field,

---

[*] The waxing moon, now as a half-moon

[†] The 15th of the month is called the 'shabattu', of the same origin as 'sabbath'.

[‡] The New Moon, which occurs when the moon lies in the same direction as the sun

[§] This specifies a year of twelve months of 30 days each.

[**] The significant lacuna here is assumed to contain a designation of 12 mansions of the moon, or something like it, which would then be constellations nearer to the horizon rather than the ecliptic: identifying the location at which the moon rises during each month throughout the year. But the only clue for this reconstruction is the preserved identification of the first as the 'Bow Star' (*Sirius*). Thus twelve reconstructed Babylonian constellations have been utilized from White (2008), with proxy associations given for each constellation based upon astrological omens, which help to illustrate but not necessarily duplicate the original contents. Also added here is the creation of the 'Star Cluster' or the *Pleiades*, the appearance of which heralded the Babylonian New Year.

Make your choice the Wild Boar for growth and productivity,

Make your choice the Mad Dog for cleansing and purification,

Make your choice the Scorpion for the overthrow of kingdoms,

Make your choice Pablisag to bring death and destruction,

Make your choice the Goatfish for disease, plague, and famine,

Let your choice be Gula as a source of wealth and prosperity,

Make your choice Lulal and Latarak for defense and security,

Make your choice the Bull of Heaven for ruin and desolation,

Make your choice the True Shepherd for revolt and occupation

Include likewise the Star Cluster for conquest and domination, [*]

The Star Cluster will rise at the time of the New Year's Festival,

Year after year it will be the most festive day among the people,

Then may all restrictions be lifted, and all ways be made clear,

The latch of the way out will be loosened to give free ingress

Beginning with these days until the coming close of seasons,

Both the watches and day and night will be properly assigned

Now will the dribble of Tiamat be the next thing to be utilized."

Marduk collected together all of the dribble that had spilled,

He collected it into clusters and made the scurrying clouds,

---

[*] These stars are *Canis Major* (Bow Star), *Argo* (Ninmah), *Crux* (Harrow), *Centaurus* (Wild Boar), *Lupus* (Mad Dog), *Scorpius* (Scorpion), *Sagittarius* (Pablisag), *Capricornus* (Goatfish), *Aquarius* (Gula), *Cetus* (Lulal & Latarak), *Taurus* (Bull of Heaven), *Orion* (True Shepherd), and *Pleiades* (Star Cluster).

Giving rise to the winds and making it a source for the rains,

By gathering together her venom, he caused mists to swell

These he managed himself, to be controlled by his own hand

He set her head out and heaped up **deep mounds of terrain**

Severing open bursting springs, from which streams poured

He made the Tigris and Euphrates rivers pour from her eyes

Sealed up her nostrils, **so that the baleful river would not flow**

He gathered together from her udder the treeless mountains

And drilled out holes so as to drain away the stagnant waters

Spanned her tail across, fixing it fast to tie up the heavens

And **established the waters of** the Apsu underneath his feet

Then he placed her thigh so as to bolster up the sky's vault

Half of her body was used to make the sky, half the earth

He **twirled** the creation, so that the insides of Tiamat spun

He spread out his net so that it spanned the entire world

Then **fixed its end points to places upon** heaven and earth

Binding them with knots after looping **them around pillars**

Then after he had set forth religion, designating its rituals,

He then tossed down the reigns, which were taken up by Ea[*]

He then took up the Tablet of Fate that Kingu had taken,

And he delivered it to Ea, to be used at the initial reading

Then the prisoners of war he'd shackled were rank-ordered;

And he marched them in enslavement before his forebears

---

[*] In other words, he relinquished his oversight which was then taken up by Ea

As for the eleven demons Tiamat had spawned, he **took them,**
Destroyed their arms, and had them bound beneath his feet,
Then he had pictures made of them and fixed at Apsu's gate,
"Let these be an indication that are recalled in future years!"

The gods all gazed, and their hearts were glad because of him
Then Lahmu, Lahamu, and his forebears clasped him fondly
And King Anshar declared they hold a celebration in his name
Then each of the gods Anu, Ellil, and Ea gave him many gifts,
And his mother Damkina likewise spoke joyous words to him;
And caused him to become bright within his splendid place
He assigned Usmu, who conveyed his gift as good tidings,
To serve as officer of the Apsu, and to manage the temples
Then the Igigi gathered and each of them bowed before him
Then every single one of the Anunnaki fell to kiss his feet
And thus the entire throng came to pay obeisance to him
Standing before him, they inclined, saying, "Truly, the King!"
The gods, his forebears, supped the full measure of the man,
Removing his ordinary clothes, besmirched with battle filth
And the gods, **his forebears,** took due care of his every need
Showering his body with **water imbued** with cypress wood
Donning a regal raiment and aspect, and a fabulous crown,
He then picked up the mace and held it in his right hand
He then picked up the scepter and held it in his left hand,
And was led by Ellil to be seated upon the imperial throne,

Who had a **foot-rest placed there to accommodate** his feet

Anu set upon **his lap the bow which had pierced Tiamat,**

And placed a rod of peace at his side, and one of obligation

When the Mantles of Brilliance **were brought before him,**

While his net was being used to hold fast dreadful Apsu,[*]

Then a bull **was led by Ea and slaughtered for the banquet**

There within the innermost chamber of his throne **room**

And within his cellar **were placed stocks of wine and liquors**

The gods and every living thing in existence **revered him,**

Lahmu and Lahamu **paid their undivided homage to him,**

They raised their voices to be heard, speaking to the Igigi,

"Until now Marduk has only been our own cherished son,

Yet now he also stands as your monarch, obey him truly!"

Then they raised their voices to be heard, speaking together,

"LUGAL-DIMMER-ANKIA is his name, put reliance in him!"[†]

And when Marduk was the recipient of their stately honors,

They declared splendid words of praise and service to him,

"From this time forward you will construct our holy temples

And everything you request of us, we will always act to fulfill!"

So Marduk raised his voice to be heard, intending to speak,

The king raised his voice to speak to his forebears, the gods,

---

[*] The task of subduing Apsu was performed by the god Ea, or Nudimmud; *supra.*

[†] This name means 'ruler of the gods of heaven and earth'.

"Above the sea-green dwelling, the Apsu, near to Esharra,
Which I made for you, after firming the earth for a temple,
There will I build my own personal abode, to solidify my rule,
At the times that you arise from the Apsu to have a congress,
Accommodating all of you, you will spend your nights there,
At the times that you descend from heaven to have a congress,
Accommodating all of you, you will spend your nights there,
From now on it will be called Babylon, the high gods' place,
And we will cause it to be the locus of all religious practices."
And his forebears, the gods, heard every word of his decree,
"None but you, sire, could have devised such a worthy thing
Who could **exceed** your **ability,** beyond what you have done?
Who could **exceed** your **works,** beyond the lands you made?
The name you have just now enunciated, which is Babylon,
We will have found there our night's lodgings, forevermore!
As for the people, they must bring to us their usual offerings,
So that man will be the one who must labor daily in the field
And for every kind of exertion that we **do for his own benefit,**
There **will the product of** his own labors **be laid before us."**
And all shouted gleefully **for the product of his great work**
The gods **will be their lords and have supremacy over** them,
Who among them knows **by what power they give** him light?
He raised his voice to be heard, making his orders **known,**
His sovereignty was to be established over them **henceforth**
He was established upon the throne of everlasting honors

And they bowed to him in praise, then the gods said to him,

Speaking their words to their Lord, Lugal-dimmer-ankia,

"Until now Marduk has only been our own cherished son,

Yet now he also stands as your monarch, obey him truly.

The god Anu bestowed unto him long life **and abundance,**

The god Ellil gave Mantles of Brilliance, mace and scepter,

The god Ea made known to him all the wisdom of the ages,

While we **dedicate ourselves to defending his rule, forever!**"

TABLET VI

Once Marduk heard the words that the gods had declared,

He was then determined to accomplish unparalleled deeds

Directing his words to Ea, of the plan he was mulling over,

"My thought is to collect blood, and construct bones also,

My thought is to create a primitive human, to be called Man

So thus I am well inclined to give rise to primal humanity

And the work which is now done by the gods, he will do,

So that the gods will not be required to labor for evermore

Through this I will alter dramatically life among the gods,

So that they might be viewed as one, even if in two camps."

Ea replied to him, and said these words to him, to Marduk,

Relating to him what he thought would bring the gods rest,

"Then have one who has been rebellious be brought forward,

That he might be slain, so that people might thus be made

And then bring together a council of all of the high gods,

Have the offender handed over, and convicted of his offence."

So thus Marduk brought together a council of the high gods,

And related to them, without trouble, the details of the plan,

Passing on his commands, and the gods listened attentively,

And they heard everything which he communicated to them

Thus the king directed his words to the Anunnaki, saying,

"The decision you have made to crown me king shall endure,

May it not be superseded! And I will forever speak the law,

And declare every statute on matters I have dominion over
Who is the one who is responsible for provoking this war,
And encouraging Tiamat to gather together a battle force?
Have this one who gave rise to the war brought before me,
So that he might be judged and sentenced for his offence,
So that you, the gods, will no longer be troubled by him."
Then the Igigi, the high gods, provided their answer to him,
To Lord Lugal-dimmer-ankia, judge of the gods, saying,
"The one you seek is Kingu, it is he who provoked this war,
It was he who encouraged Tiamat to gather a battle force!"
And thus they chained him and brought him before Ea,
And they judged and sentenced him, and spilled his blood
From this Ea made humankind, from out of his lost blood[*]
To him they gave the labor of the gods, thus freeing them
Then after the knowledgeable Ea had made humankind,
He had him do the labor of the gods, a deed beyond words,
For Nudimmud did it with the wondrous power of Marduk

King Marduk then caused the gods to be separated into two,
Each of the Anunnaki was to be assigned above or beneath
And he spoke a pronouncement that Anu be the guardian,
And designated three-hundred gods to guard the heavens

---

[*] Thus Kingu in his rebellion is not unlike Satan, and so this becomes the source of the innate 'rebelliousness' within mankind. (see George 2003: xl-xliii)

Then did just the same in his declaration concerning earth,
So that the entire six-hundred resided on earth or in heaven

Then after he had finished making all of his declarations,
Having made the Anunnaki reside in either heaven or earth,
The Anunnaki raised their voices to Lord Marduk, saying,
"Since you have now liberated us from our work, O Lord,
What manner of kindnesses might you now bestow unto us?
For we would like to construct a temple of great distinction,
To have our sleeping quarters alongside yours, so as to rest,
Thus permit us to build a temple where we might find shelter,
So that whenever we gather to you, we might lounge there."
Once Marduk heard their words, his face shone like sunlight,
"Then build Babylon, to be the construction project you seek!
Have there be mud-bricks cast, and construct a lofty temple!"
Thus the Anunnaki excavated, making bricks for a full year,
And when the following year came, they had erected it high,
Raising aloft the peak of Esagila, which was nearby the Apsu;
Thus they had constructed a lofty ziggurat fit for the Apsu[*]
There were also built places of residence for Anu, Ellil, and Ea
Highest among any edifice, it was established before them,
Where its towers gaze down upon the foundations of Esharra
After they had completed their work on the temple Esagila,

---

[*] Thus the ziggurat of Babylon, or the 'Tower of Babel'

Tablet VI

And each of the Anunnaki made his own personal temple,
Then the three-hundred Igigi gods, who inhabited heaven,
Together with the Anunnaki gods of the Apsu, came together
Then the Lord invited his forebears, the gods, to a feast,
There in the vast palace he had made as his own residence,
"Truly, this 'Gate of God' will now likewise be your home!
And so let there be singing and festivity, and be content!"
Thus the high gods took their places there at the tables,
Beer mugs were set out, and they took part in the banquet
Then after having enjoyed themselves there for some time,
They all went to grand Esagila to make a show-offering

Thus every one of these orders and aims were established
And each god had been given a place in heaven or on earth
And fifty high gods set forth the seven echelons of the cult
And the Lord took his bow up and placed it before them,
His forebears, the gods, also examined the net he had made,
Inspecting the bow, gazing upon its wondrous workmanship,
And his forebears extolled all of his fine accomplishments
Then Anu lifted her up and addressed the divine council,
Kissing the bow, and saying, "Let her have unrivaled range!"[*]
And declared for the bow what she would be called, saying,

---

[*] This phrase, also meaning 'she will be my daughter', is a reference to the goddess Ishtar, Anu's daughter, associated too with the Bow Star. (Dalley 2000: 276)

41

"Thus ought 'Long and Far' be primary, 'Victory' secondary,
And her third name is 'Bow Star', for its glow in the heavens."
And he secured her a place amongst her associates, the gods,
Then after Anu had declared the rank of the bow henceforth,
He located her throne, "Of all gods your place will be highest!"
Anu caused her to be seated at the divine council of the gods
The high gods congregated and made Marduk foremost of all
Bowing themselves before him, they swore oaths of allegiance,
And it was sworn by water and oil, motioning to their necks,[*]
In doing so they thus affirmed that he be the gods' overlord,
And certified his rule over every god in both heaven and earth

Then Anshar declared that Marduk be known as ASARLUHI,
"Then when his name is pronounced we will all bow ourselves!
And the gods are well advised to give due notice to his words
His declarations shall have precedence both above and beneath,
And there will be none higher than the son who is our avenger!
With his authority second to none, he shall have no challenger!
He will be a shepherd to the entire people of his own making,
May all his acts be spoken of in the future, never to be forsaken
He will begin the grand food-offering in honor of his forebears
He will be their guardian, and will be protector of their temples
He will cause them to breathe deeply of the smoke-offering,

---

[*] Probably a reference to suffering punishment by beheading if they did not honor their oath

As such he will cause their utterances to be joyous and mirthful
May his breath be as freely taken on earth as it is in heaven
May he cause the entire people of earth to give him reverence,
So that humankind will remember him, and call him their god
May their mediating goddess give heed whenever he speaks,
May these food-offerings be made to both god and goddess
So that they never be forsaken! So that they abide by their god
So their nation is supreme, never ceasing from erecting temples
Even as the entire people each chooses his own among the gods
For us, under whatever name he might be called, he is our god!

So gather round, and let us all call him by all his fifty names!
May all his manners be recalled in the future, all he does also!
MARDUK — as Anu, his father, chose at the time he was born
To guard pastures, lakes, and springs; so that herds increase,
Who overpowered the rebels with his awesome Flood-weapon
And released his forebears, the gods, from their anguishes
May his name be declared to be 'The Son, King of the Gods!'
Might they walk henceforth in the glow of his pervading aura,
The humans that he made of mortal life, who must breathe,
He set them to do the gods' work, that they might have leisure
Both creation and obliteration, both sentence and absolution,
These he might always call upon, so they ought to defer to him
MARUKKA — is the name of the god that made humankind
Bringing blessings to the Anunnaki, freeing the Igigi from toil

MARUTUKKU — is benefactor of the land, town, and people

He is the one that humankind will give reverence for all time

MERSHAKUSHU — is severe but kind, forceful but forgiving

He is magnanimous of heart, and is not ruled by his emotions

LUGAL-DIMMER-ANKIA — the name we gave him together

His decrees we made superior to those of his forebears, the gods

There is no doubt he is BEL of every god of heaven and earth, [*]

A king whose words are revered by the gods above and beneath

NARI-LUGAL-DIMMER-ANKIA — is his name as leader of gods,

Who gave us homes in heaven and earth, despite the challenges,

And who assigned the various duties of the Igigi and Anunnaki

At the utterance of his names the gods rightly shudder at home

ASARLUHI — is the name given to him by his grandfather Anu [†]

May he provide guidance to the gods, and be the best chief,

Who, true to his name, is guardian of both divinity and nation,

Saving our homes from the tide of war, despite the challenges

Also, they refer to Asarluhi as NAMTILA, given he is god of life

He healed each of the injured gods as though he'd made them

He is Bel, who brings the dead gods back with his perfect spell,

Defeating all his challengers, and **conquering all** his enemies

The third name of Asarluhi is NAMRU, given for this reason:

He is the god of purity who cleanses the pathways before us."

---

[*] Bel means 'Lord'

[†] Asarluhi means 'first'

Tablet VI

Anshar, Lahmu, and Lahamu shouted out his three names;
They declared them openly before all their children, the gods,
"We have designated him to be known by these three names,
So then you too must shout these names out just as we have!"
And the gods were pleased and did as they were commanded
In Ubshu-ukkinakku there was a discussion in their assembly,
"We ought to do something to honor the son, the hero's name,
Him who is our defender, and is our guardian and savior!"
They took seats at the council and started to proclaim fates
And they voiced his name during every one of their rituals

TABLET VII

"ASARE, giver of farmland, and he who defines its limits
Inventor of cereals and flaxseed, who brings plant growth
ASAR-ALIM, whose sage words of advice are well regarded
Within the Hall of the Congress, esteemed above all others,
Among the gods, even the fearless ones give heed to him
ASAR-ALIM-NUNA, who is much honored and praised,
Who is the shining light of his forebears, his progenitors,
Who manages the decrees of Anu, Ellil, Ea, and Damkina
Yes, it is he who sustains them, and gives them livelihood,
His own farm provides enough to bring surplus to the land

He is known as TUTU, having brought their restoration
And he will cleanse their temples that they need not work
And he will create a spell so that the gods will live in peace
If any of them should become enraged, he will quell him
He will be utmost at the congress of his forebears, the gods
And there will emerge no god who could surmount him
He as Tutu is also ZI-UKKINA, who enlightens his people
Who set firmly into place the flawless heaven for the gods,
Who determined their manner and established their order
Let him not ever be forsaken by the multitude of humanity
So that they may always recall all of his accomplishments
Tutu is thirdly known as ZIKU, who insists upon cleanliness

God of sweet scents, and lord of adherence and agreement,

Giver of wealth and plenty, who produces beyond his needs,

He who can transform short supply into great abundance

When beset by the worst calamity, we smell his sweetness!

Let them speak utterances of praise and glorify him in song!

Fourth, may humankind worship Tutu by the name AGAKU,

He being lord of the immaculate spell, bringing resurrection

He is compassionate even to the gods who are captives of war

He relieved the burden placed upon the gods, even his rivals,

He who made humankind to release them from their labors,

Being filled with blessings, and one who can bring even life!

He will speak words as durable as stone that will not be lost

When the body of people speak, who he made with his hands

Fifth, they will refer to Tutu as TUKU, of flawless incantations,

Eradicating all the malevolent through his immaculate spell

Call him SHAZU, fully aware of the gods' plans and feelings

He will not permit the workers of evil to flee from his clutches,

Founder of the divine council, who fulfills what pleases them,

Bringing the haughty to their knees under his broad shelter

Overseer of justice, and who recognizes deception in speech,

And from where he plainly differentiates a lie from the truth

Let them also praise Shazu as ZISI, who stifles the aggressive,

Who banishes doom from the bodies of his forebears, the gods

Third, Shazu is SUHRIM, who eradicates all enemies in war,

Bringing an end to their plans, banishing them far and wide,
Bringing an end to all who are evil, no matter where they are
That the gathered gods may forever remember his victories!
Fourth, he as Shazu should too be known as SUHGURIM,
Having charge of the compliance of his forebears, the gods
Who eradicates the enemy and obliterates their descendants
Who ended their designs, so that nothing remained of them
May his name be praised and declared throughout the land
Fifth, let the descendants of man know Shazu as ZAHIRIM,
Who brings every enemy, given to haughtiness, to an end
And all the gods, who had been driven out, to their temples
So may it be instituted, that he might be known by this name
Sixth, have them all likewise worship Shazu as ZAHGURIM,
Who brought an end to every enemy by his fortitude in war

Call him ENBILULU, the master, and the bringer of wealth;
They have a potent god, who rules the portents of sacrifice,
Who guards pastures, lakes, and springs; for the land's sake
Who releases springs and gives out water in plentiful supply
Second, they ought to know Enbilulu likewise as EPADUN,
As the master of the land and farming, bringer of furrows,
Who manages the canals which are in both heaven and earth
Who sustains the unsullied farmland throughout the country
Who makes the trenches and canals flow, and makes furrows

Third, to praise Enbilulu as GUGAL of irrigation of the gods[*]

And Lord of plentitude and the abundances of heaping grain

Who brings about wealth, who distributes his excess to others,

As the provider of grains, and as the cultivator of cereal crops

Fourth, that he as Enbilulu is also known by them as HEGAL,[†]

As he who gathers into piles the spare supply for the people,

Who is the provider of plentiful rains across the wide earth,

And who brings about the burgeoning of all vegetative life

He is called SIRSIR, who heaped the mountains atop Tiamat,

Who captured, among the spoils of war, the cadaver of Tiamat

He is ruler of the land, and is likewise their good shepherd,

Who has given freely agriculture, garden land, and plow land

Who struck out into the wide Sea of Tiamat, when provoked

And he was spread over the entire field of battle, like a bridge

Second, that Sirsir is known as MALAH, and let her, Tiamat,[‡]

Act as his barge from henceforth, and let him be her boatman

He is called GIL, who collects great piles and masses of grains,

Bringing both grain and herds; supplier of the land's fertility

He is called GILIMA, for the divine force binding the cosmos,

---

[*] Gugal means 'canal manager'

[†] Hegal means 'plenty'

[‡] Malah means 'boatman'

He brought order, the encircling band, which brings goodness
He is called high AGLIMA, who banished the flood and frost,
Made the land sit upon the waters, and formed soaring peaks[*]
He is called ZULUM, who assigned plots of land for the gods,
Who divvied up what he had made, and bestowed temples,
Acting as both the giver of livelihood and the supplier of food,
He is called MUMMU, the maker of both heaven and earth,
Serving as controller of **their forces, instiller of their energies**
And ZULUM-UMMU, as god who purges heaven and earth,
There are none among the divinities who equal him in might

He is called GISH-NUMUN-AB, the one who made humanity,
And who likewise established the four divisions of the earth,
Who ended Tiamat's divine force, and made man exclusively
He is likewise known as the monarch, LUGAL-AB-DUBUR,
Who dispersed the offspring of Tiamat, and took her weapon
He put fortitude into both the rearguard and the vanguard
He is PAGAL-GUENA, chief of lords, of unsurpassed power
Being matchless among his kinsmen, the gods; their prince
He is LUGAL-DURMAH, the sovereign, and the divine force,
And is likewise the lord of the binding force of the cosmos,
Being second to none in the palace; indisputably supreme

---

[*] Compare with II Esdras 16:58 – 'He hath shut the sea in the midst of the waters, and with his word hath he hanged the earth upon the waters.'

He is ARANINA, Ea's advisor, rock of his forebears, the gods,

Who remains unsurpassed in every one of his regal manners

He is DUMU-DUKU, whose pristine house sits on a holy hill,

Judgement would not be without Dumu-duku, LUGAL-DUKU

He is king LUGAL-SHUANNA, of unrivalled divine influence

Lord, strength of Anu, foremost as the rightful heir of Anshar

He is IRUGA, who set forth to draw them from Tiamat's sway

Who unifies all wisdom, and holds a comprehensive insight

Call him IRKINGU, since he made Kingu a prisoner of war,

He pronounces rulings for all, and proclaims imperatives

Call him KINMA, as ruler of all gods and source of wisdom,

His uttered name makes gods shudder like an earthquake

Named E-SIZKUR, he has the foremost place at the temple,

The gods will arrive bringing gifts to place before his feet,

For as long as he accepts the dedications they give to him

There are none who could do sorcery without his backing

No other god will determine what is due the entire people,

Apart from his aid; nor the designation of their life-spans

Call him GIBIL, who determines the **effectiveness** of arms,

He who worked wonders in his confrontation with Tiamat

Of deepest wisdom, and supreme in his comprehensions,

So deep it is beyond the grasp of other gods to understand

His name will be ADDU, may he forever span the heavens,

Let his tremendous voice be heard booming above the earth

Let him discharge the rains which fall freely from the clouds,

Enuma Elish

Which are the source of nourishment for humanity beneath
He is ASHARU, who, true to his name, rules the gods of Fate;
Truly he watches over every living person who lives on earth

Call him NEBERU, who secures the ways of heaven and earth
Neither up nor down will they pass, but only with his consent
His star is Neberu, which is a dazzling light in the firmament
He secures the passages, thus they must seek his permission,
Saying, 'He who incessantly passed within Tiamat without stop
Will carry the name of Neberu, for holding fast at her center
Let him be the one who sets the stars of heaven on their way,
Let him be the shepherd of the gods, who will be his sheep
May he bring down Tiamat, strangle her and end her days
So, until the end of time, she remains far from our children.'
Since he was the one who both made the heavens and earth,
Call him ENKURKUR, which his forebear Ellil called him,
Ea heard this name, and he was so known among the Igigi
And Ea was overcome with happiness, and spoke, saying,
'He who has been given such a fine name by his forebears,
Deserves to be known by the name 'Ea', being my own name
He will rule over the particulars of every one of my rituals,
And will administer any matter which I have proclaimed.'"

Thus with these fifty did the high gods give his fifty names,
Granting him preeminence; may they always be honored!

And might the elder enlighten the younger concerning them

May men of wisdom and instruction talk among themselves,

So the father might recall them, and pass them on to his son

And may both the shepherd and the herdsman be amenable,

That he not forget the wise counselor of the gods, Marduk,

So that his lands will remain productive, and himself secure

He speaks words of stone, and commands beyond reproach

There are none among the gods who should alter his words

Even when overcome with anger, he does not avert his gaze;

But in his greatest ferocity and annoyance, the gods back off

His thinking is profound, and his feelings highly developed;

Both criminals and offenders are made to stand before him

And he had a scribe transcribe the unwritten commandments,

That had been repeated to him by the elderly amongst them,

Having this set forth in writing for men to read into the future

Might mankind, **the people** of Marduk, made by the Igigi gods,

Invoke the **story**, utter his name, recalling the Song of Marduk

Of him who struck down mighty Tiamat, and was made king!

ATRAHASIS

TABLET 1

When gods, not men, performed the work, bore the burdens
The weight was too great, the work too taxing, a sore plight
So the seven great Anunnaki made the Igigi to take the load
The king was their father, Anu; their counselor of war, Ellil,
The chamberlain, Nimrod; and their canal manager, Ennugi,
Taking up the container they cast lots, the gods divvied up,
So that Anu took his home in the heavens, to live in the sky
While Ellil went to make his abode among the men of earth
And astute Enki acquired for himself the entire sea's crater
After Anu was in the sky, and the Apsu gods did descend,
Then the heavenly Anunnaki made the Igigi take the load
They caused the gods to carve out the many water canals
They had to open up conduits, the sustenance of the land
They caused the Igigi to carve out the many water canals
They had to open up conduits, the sustenance of the land
So the immortals carved out the channel of the river Tigris
And the divinities carved out the channel of the Euphrates
Boring a chamber at the lowest depths, setting **stanchions**
In the deep waters of the Apsu, **beneath a covering** of land
They placed braces within, **situating these to** raise it aloft,
Those which stand at the peaks, underlying all mountains
And they kept track of every long year that they worked

57

Atrahasis

The excess water drained down to fill up the great swamp
And they kept track of every long year that they worked

It was 3,600 years in which they carried the heavy loads,
The work was burdensome; they were busy night and day
So they grumbled and blamed one another often enough,
They complained over the piles of soil they had dug up,
"We should go to the chamberlain, to our **chief overseer,**
So that he might bring us rest from our unrelenting labors!
Let us go and bring out **the lord,** as the supreme authority,
As the counselor of war, bring him forth out of his house,
Let us go there and collect Ellil, as the supreme authority,
As the counselor of war, bring him forth out of his house."
Among them Alla raised his voice to speak and be heard
Making a speech to his brothers, to all of the high gods,
"We've kept track of every long year that we've worked
It has been 3,600 years we have carried the heavy loads,
The work is burdensome; we remain busy night and day
So we've grumbled and blamed one another often enough,
We complain over the piles of soil that we have dug up,
We should go to the chamberlain, to our chief overseer,
So that he might bring us rest from our unrelenting labors!
Let us go and bring out the lord, as the supreme authority,
As the counselor of war, bring him forth out of his house,
Let us go there and collect Ellil, as the supreme authority,

As the counselor of war, bring him forth out of his house
So let us raise up our battle cry and bring war to the fore!"
The gods listened to every word as he made his speech,
They placed their implements in piles and set them aflame
Their troubles dispatched to the fire god, consumed in fire
When they arrived at the gate of Ellil, wise war counselor,
It was already nighttime; it was already the middle watch
His house was already encircled, but the god did not know
It was already nighttime; it was already the middle watch,
Ekur had already been encircled, but Ellil did not know it
But his servant Kalkal had the good sense to close the gate
He secured the lock and then kept an eye on the entryway
Kalkal went and woke Nusku, and they observed the Igigi,
Nusku then went to wake up his lord, got him out of bed,
"Master, you must know that your house is surrounded,
And a raucous mob has already gathered about your door!
Master Ellil, you must know your house is surrounded,
And a raucous mob has already gathered about your door!"
So Ellil had weapons he kept for his residence brought out
Ellil raised his voice to be heard, saying to his officer Nusku,
"Nusku, first you must go and suitably secure the door,
Then pick up your weapons and set yourself before me."
So Nusku went and sought to suitably secure the door,
Then picked up his weapons and took his place before Ellil
Nusku raised his voice to be heard, speaking to chief Ellil,

"My lord, behold your face has become pale as a tamarisk!
For what reason do you show such fear of your own clan?
Ellil, behold, your face has become pale as a tamarisk tree!
For what reason do you show such fear of your own clan?
Make an announcement that Anu might come to your aid,
And do so that Enki will have cause to stand by your side."
So a herald was sent with word that Anu might come to him,
And so that Enki had cause to journey and stand at his side,
So that now the king of the wide heavens, Anu, had arrived,
And so too the king of the mighty abyss, Enki was there too
Also, there gathered the great Anunnaki to be in attendance
Ellil stood up to make his case, raising his voice to be heard,
He spoke to the entire assembly of the high gods gathered,
"Have they raised up in armed rebellion so as to depose me?
Ought I now raise my weapons **to go against my own clan?**
For what did I behold here with my own eyes when I looked,
But that there was an angry mob assembled about my door!"

Anu raised his voice to be heard, speaking to the chief Ellil,
"Then command Nusku to go, to divine the Igigi's purpose
Have him establish the will of those gathered at your door
A word from you **and this whole thing could be cleared up**
To **find out for what reason they have gathered at your door."**
Ellil raised his voice to be heard, saying to his officer Nusku,
"Nusku, go first to open the door, then pick up your weapons

Tablet I

And take your place before me! Then go out among the gods
First prostrate yourself, then rise up and speak to them thus:
'Your father Anu, supreme authority Ellil, the lord Nimrod,
And the manager of your canals Ennugi, wish me to request:
Who is the one among you who is leader of this heated mob?
Who is the one among you who is organizer of this uprising?
Who among you has turned his face unto the arena of war?
Who are you that have come here hastily to the door of Ellil?'"
So Nusku went and opened the door, picked up his weapons
Then took his place before Ellil, in the presence of the gods
After prostrating himself, he rose and spoke to them thusly,
"Your father Anu, supreme authority Ellil, the lord Nimrod,
And the manager of your canals Ennugi, wish me to request:
Who is the one among you who is leader of this heated mob?
Who is the one among you who is organizer of this uprising?
Who among you has turned his face unto the arena of war?
Who are you that have come here hastily to the door of Ellil?"
Thus Nusku spoke to carry out the duty given to him by Ellil
Now Alla raised his voice to be heard, speaking to Nusku,
"Every one of the gods is ready to come to blows over this!
And we have thus stopped partaking in our endless digging,
The burden is far too heavy for us, and it was diminishing us
The weight is very great, the work too taxing, a sore plight!
And so each god sought to bring his discontent before Ellil."
Nusku hefted up his weapons, turned and came back to Ellil

"My lord, I performed my mission to disclose the situation
I went to find an answer as to why your door is surrounded
Having explicated the things you gave me charge to convey,
This then is what response they gave me in reply; they said,
'Every one of the gods is ready to come to blows over this!
And we have thus stopped partaking in our endless digging,
The burden is far too heavy for us, and it was diminishing us
The weight is very great, the work too taxing, a sore plight!
And so each god sought to bring his discontent before Ellil.'"
So Ellil listened to everything he said, and became tearful,
Ellil chose words with care, speaking to the conqueror Anu,
"Wise judge, return with this verdict to your heavenly realm
Flex your muscles before the Anunnaki gathered about you,
Declare one god from among them, allocate him to perish!"
Anu raised his voice to be heard, speaking to his fellow gods,
"For what reason would we have to criticize their complaints,
The weight was too great, the work too taxing, a sore plight!
Every day the earth re-echoed the sounds of their agonies
This was a warning which we all heard, it was clear enough,
There is only one course open to us, and a single thing to do
We must create a creature who can carry the burden of gods
When you are there with the Anunnaki gathered around you,
And so too is Belet-ili the womb-goddess in your presence,
Declare one of the gods among them, allocate him to perish!"

Anu raised his voice to be heard, saying to his officer Nusku,

"Nusku, go first to open the door, and pick up your weapons

Then go out and prostrate yourself before the gathered gods

Then rise and raise your voice **to be heard, and say to them:**

'Your father Anu, supreme authority Ellil, the lord Nimrod,

And the manager of your canals Ennugi, wish me to request,

Who is the one among you who is leader of this heated mob?

Who is the one among you who is organizer of this uprising?

Who among you has turned his face unto the arena of war?

Who are you that have come here hastily to the door of Ellil?'"

So when Nusku heard everything, he picked up his weapons,

Then after prostrating himself before the gathering of gods,

He rose, and raising his voice **to be heard, said this to them,**

"Anu, your father, supreme authority Ellil, the lord Nimrod,

And the manager of your canals Ennugi, wish me to request,

Who is the one among you who is leader of this heated mob?

Who is the one among you who is organizer of this uprising?

Who among you has turned his face unto the arena of war?

Who are you that have come here hastily to the door of Ellil?"

[This Nusku spoke to carry out the duty given to him by Ellil

Now Alla raised his voice to be heard, speaking to Nusku,

"Every one of the gods is ready to come to blows over this!

And we have thus stopped partaking in our endless digging,

The burden is far too heavy for us, and it was diminishing us

The weight is very great, the work too taxing, a sore plight!

And so each god sought to bring his discontent before Ellil."
Nusku hefted up his weapons, turned and came back to Ellil
"My lord, I performed my mission to disclose the situation
I went to find an answer as to why your door is surrounded
Having explicated the things you gave me charge to convey,
This then is what response they gave me in reply; they said,
'Every one of the gods is ready to come to blows over this!
And we have thus stopped partaking in our endless digging,
The burden is far too heavy for us, and it was diminishing us
The weight is very great, the work too taxing, a sore plight!
And so each god sought to bring his discontent before Ellil.'"
So Ellil listened to everything he said, and became tearful,
Ellil chose words with care, speaking to the combatant Anu,
"Wise judge, return with this verdict to your heavenly realm
Flex your muscles before the Anunnaki gathered about you,
Declare one god from among them, allocate him to perish!"]
Ea raised his voice to be heard, speaking to his brother gods,
"For what reason would we have to criticize their complaints,
The weight was too great, the work too taxing, a sore plight!
Every day the earth **re-echoed the sounds of their agonies**
This was a warning which we all heard, it was clear enough,
There is **only one course open to us, and a single thing to** do
(We must create a creature who can carry the burden of gods)
Belet-ili the womb-goddess is here to make a primitive man
That he be made to bear the yoke and to carry the burdens

[Let him be the one to bear the yoke, who does Ellil's work,
And so man will be the one who performs the labor of gods!"

Ea raised his voice to be heard, saying to his officer Nusku,
"Nusku, go first to open the door, and pick up your weapons
Then go out and prostrate yourself before the gathered gods
Then rise and raise your voice to be heard, and say to them:
'Your father Anu, supreme authority Ellil, the lord Nimrod,
And the manager of your canals Ennugi, wish me to request:
Who is the one among you who is leader of this heated mob?
Who is the one among you who is organizer of this uprising?
Who among you has turned his face unto the arena of war?
Who are you that have come here hastily to the door of Ellil?'"
So when Nusku heard everything, he picked up his weapons,
Then after prostrating himself before the gathering of gods
He rose, and raising his voice to be heard, said this to them,
"Anu, your father, supreme authority Ellil, the lord Nimrod,
And the manager of your canals Ennugi, wish me to request:
Who is the one among you who is leader of this heated mob?
Who is the one among you who is organizer of this uprising?
Who among you has turned his face unto the arena of war?
Who are you that have come here hastily to the door of Ellil?"
This Nusku spoke to carry out the duty given to him by Ellil
Now Alla raised his voice to be heard, speaking to Nusku,
"Every one of the gods is ready to come to blows over this!

And we have thus stopped partaking in our endless digging,
The burden is far too heavy for us, and it was diminishing us
The weight is very great, the work too taxing, a sore plight!
And so each god sought to bring his discontent before Ellil."
Nusku hefted up his weapons, turned and came back to Ellil
"My lord, I performed my mission to disclose the situation
I went to find an answer as to why your door is surrounded
Having explicated the things you gave me charge to convey,
This then is what response they gave me in reply; they said,
'Every one of the gods is ready to come to blows over this!
And we have thus stopped partaking in our endless digging,
The burden is far too heavy for us, and it was diminishing us
The weight is very great, the work too taxing, a sore plight!
And so each god sought to bring his discontent before Ellil.'"
So Ellil listened to everything he said, and became tearful,
Ellil chose words with care, speaking to the combatant Anu,
"Wise judge, return with this verdict to your heavenly realm
Flex your muscles before the Anunnaki gathered about you,
Declare one god from among them, allocate him to perish!"]
Ellil raised his voice to be heard, speaking to his brother gods,
["For what reason would we have to criticize their complaints,
The weight was too great, the work too taxing, a sore plight!
Every day the earth re-echoed the sounds of their agonies
This was a warning which we all heard, it was clear enough,
There is only one course open to us, and a single thing to do

We must create a creature who can carry the burden of gods]
Belet-ili the womb-goddess is here, have her bear offspring
That man will be the one who performs the labor of gods!"

They called the goddess, the midwife, shrewd Mami, saying,
"You are the womb-goddess, give rise to the species of man!
Give rise to a primitive human, to perform the labor of gods!
Let him be the one to bear the yoke, who does Ellil's work,
So that man will be the one who performs the labor of gods!"
Nintu raised her voice to be heard, speaking to the high gods,
"It is not best that I fashion him, this is better done by Enki[*]
For it is by his efforts that things are made free from error
But if he provides me with clay, I will certainly carry it out."
Enki raised his voice to be heard, speaking to the high gods,
"Know that on the first, seventh, and fifteenth of the month
I will conduct a water-purification, and one god will be slain
Thus the gods will be cleansed through these holy ablutions
Then Nintu will combine the clay with his flesh and blood
So that a being, divine and mortal, will come from the clay
Then we will hear the heart-beat rhythms from henceforth
Let the spirit arise into being from out of the divine flesh,
But let her relate to man, while he is alive, of his condition
So they will never forget that the spirit is eternally made."

---

[*] Enki is another name for Ea, the water god.

And all gathered in the assemblage gave their affirmation,
Of the holy Anunnaki who were the determiners of destiny
Then it was on the first, seventh, and fifteenth of the month
That he conducted a water-purification through immersion
The wise god Ilawela was chosen to be slain at the congress
Nintu combined together the clay with his flesh and blood
So that they heard the heart-beat rhythms from henceforth
And the spirit arose into being from out of the divine flesh,
Nintu related to man, while he was alive, of his condition
So they would never forget that the spirit is eternally made
Then after having done this she combined together the clay,
Then she convened the high gods, both Anunnaki and Igigi
And she caused her spittle to dribble onto the heap of clay
Then Mami raised her voice, speaking to the high gods,
"I have done precisely the task that was given to me to do
And you have slain a god altogether along with his mind
Now I have brought you release from your tiresome tasks
And have caused your burdens to be shifted onto mankind
While you have given humanity the capacity for speaking
Thus I have released the bonds and brought you freedom!"
Hearing every word spoken with relief, they kissed her feet
"Until now we have referred to you by the name of Mami,
But henceforth you shall be called 'Mistress of all the Gods!'"
Then astute Enki and wise Mami went to the abode of Fate
There the womb-goddesses had already gathered together

And there he stomped upon the clay pile while she stood by
So she chanted the spells Enki, who was there, asked her to
When she had finished, she pulled off fourteen bits of clay
Setting out seven bits on her right and seven bits on her left,
And midway between the columns she set there a mud-brick
And then she slit open a stiff reed and severed the umbilical
Then called over the clever and worldly womb-goddesses,
Here, seven and seven, were seven males and seven females,
For the womb-goddesses were the determiners of destiny
So he **covered** each pair, Enki **covered** them, as she looked
And Mami set forth the following customs for the people:
Within the dwelling of the woman who is the one bearing,
Then shall the mud-brick be placed there for seven full days
Then there will be a tribute to Belet-ili, the sagacious Mami,
And joy in the midwife's heart within the new mother's home
After bearing her baby, then the mother will separate herself
Thus the man **will be paired** with the girl, **who is yet a virgin,**
Only after maturing, when her bosom **has fully developed,**
And when the young man's beard is seen upon his cheek
Within the gardens and paths will she find her husband."
And the womb-goddess came together there with Nintu,
And they counted every one of the months as they went by
Assigning the tenth month to be the designated duration
Then after one full term, upon arrival of the tenth month,
She would deftly manage a measure and open the womb

And her expression would be one of joy and satisfaction
And she would drape her head and take the role of midwife
She would then secure her belt, and speak aloud a blessing
Then spread flour into a picture, and set out a mud-brick
"I was the one who created, my hands the ones which made
The midwife will be joyous in the nursing-priestess's house
Anywhere a woman gives birth, and the mother is separated,
Then there shall the mud-brick be placed for fully nine days
And the womb-goddess Nintu shall receive her due honors
Then she will utter **the name of their undying mother** 'Mami'
And likewise will **she speak the name of** the womb-goddess,
And spread out a cloth of linen when the house bed is made

The wife and the husband will select each other for partners
And Ishtar will be gladdened by the wedding of man and wife,
Where it will take place within the dwelling of the father-in-law
And there shall be celebrations which last for fully nine days
Where they will call upon Princess Ishtar by the name 'Ishhara'
Then on the fifteenth day, as has been determined by destiny,
She will call **the bride and the groom together to the bridal bed**[9]
The man and wife will then live together, bound to one another
And shall carry out the work for their existence, acting in virtue
Never straying from the honorable, bringing the gifts of gods,
To live according to the ways established for them by the gods:

70

To live free from adulterous acts or satisfying homosexuality,[*]
To live free from shameful acts or what brings hands to guilt
Do not attain your wealth unduly, but gain by upright means
Be satisfied with your own things and do not take from others
Do not engage in deceit, but declare all truthfully and honestly
Above all honor the gods, and after them honor your parents
Perform labors so you can manage through your own efforts,
Because the one who is idle makes his livelihood from stealing
Learning a skill gives a man his living, the slothful go hungry
Do not find yourself eating what another man has left behind,
Rather obtain your food properly from the fruit of your labors
But if he fails to acquire a skill, in its place he must ply the hoe
There is no shortage of work for one who is agreeable to labor
Become a marine merchant, if wishing to sail; the seas are vast
If you prefer to plow cultivatable land, the countryside is wide
Nothing worthwhile comes without toil, for men or for gods
Likewise, through work one enlarges his own righteousness

When ants leave their nests, unseen deep within the earth,
Driven by their requirement that they provender themselves,
When the field has filled the threshing floor with its bounty
After reaping, they carry loads of the newly threshed grain

---

[*] These 28 lines are from Pseudo-Phocylides (3-8, 153-174), provided as a vague substitute for the absent instructional lines.

Be it wheat or barley, one hauler follows behind the other,

It is from summer's harvest that they stock up winter's food

Not given to rest, these minute ones do a fair share of labor

While too the bee works, through the air, toiling tirelessly,

Be it within the cleft of an empty rock or amongst reed-beds,

Or be it within an old hollow oak tree; there inside their nests,

Swarming in their combs of innumerable cells, making wax

Thus man will seek his work and continue until the twilight

Prepare the home for his arrival, when his day's work is done

The father's son learns this from him, remaining at his side."

The gods went out to look upon the tasks being done nearby

They remained there a while and then went to the god Ellil,

And he gathered up the things which were required to forge

He then saw the father and his son and walked up to them

Ellil showed them the way to smelt iron and to work steel

And they took up the metal implements from the ash pile

From these they produced new picks and spades to utilize

To dig long channels to provide food and please the gods[10]

And the water fed the lands well, food became abundant

People harvested their fields of grain, made bread, and ate,

They performed then for the first time the many sacrifices:

So they prepared a flour-offering to the gods, their patrons

And they prepared a food-offering to the gods, their patrons

They prepared a present-offering to the gods, their patrons

They prepared a show-offering for the gods, their patrons

They prepared a smoke-offering to the gods, their patrons
They prepared a disperse-offering to the gods, their patrons
They prepared an incense-offering to the gods, their patrons
In addition to this they made their daily sacrifices to the gods
And the gods enjoyed their offerings, and were contented
But man gathered, going about their business in the towns
They ate their bread and drank their beer and had offspring
And their numbers became more and more; greater by far

Six-hundred years, not even six-hundred years went by
The inhabited land sprawled and the people grew plentiful
And the inhabited lands raised a howl like a bellowing bull
But the god was annoyed by all the noise that they made
Ellil had to put up with all of their loud clamor and clatter
Ellil raised his voice to be heard, speaking to the high gods,
"The noise which is made by man has become too great,
All of this clamor and clatter has kept me from my sleep
Therefore command an outbreak of the shivering disease
And thus the divine Namtara was summoned by the gods
Then the divine Namtara unleashed the shivering disease,
And all of the people were beset by the plague outbreak
There was one man among them who was named Atrahasis
And he heeded diligently the words spoken by his god Enki
He often communed with his god, receiving the god's reply
Atrahasis raised his voice to be heard, speaking to his lord,

"How long are we going to be **beset by this terrible disease?**
Is it their intention that we bear this syndrome for all time?"
Enki raised his voice to be heard, speaking to his servant,
"Bring together the elders; gather to you the men of rank
So as to instigate a rebellion within your own community!
Send out messengers to announce this within every district
And cause them to raise a loud cry throughout all lands
That you no longer will pay fitting homage to your gods
That you no longer beseech the favor of your goddesses
But rather find your way to the door of the god Namtara
Present him a loaf of baked bread, leave a flour offering,
And let him feel his own shame upon receiving these gifts
So that he might remove from you his discredited hand."[*]
Atrahasis did as he was told, bringing the elders to his door
And he raised his voice to be heard, speaking to the elders,
"I have brought together the elders, and the men of rank,
So as to instigate a rebellion within our own community
Send out messengers to announce this within every district
And cause them to raise a loud cry throughout all lands
That you no longer will pay fitting homage to your gods
That you no longer beseech the favor of your goddesses
But rather find your way to the door of the god Namtara
Present him a loaf of baked bread, leave a flour offering

---

[*] The hand of the god, meaning his influence, the plague

And let him feel his own shame upon receiving these gifts
That he might remove from off of us his discredited hand."
And the elders paid heed to his prudently spoken advice
Thus they built a temple in the city dedicated to Namtara,
Sent out messengers to announce this within every district
And caused them to raise a loud cry throughout all lands
So they no longer would pay fitting homage to their gods
So they no longer beseeched the favor of their goddesses
But rather found their way to the door of the god Namtara
Presented him a loaf of baked bread, left a flour offering,
Such that he himself felt shame upon receiving these gifts
So that he removed from off of them his discredited hand
And the shivering disease was no longer a menace to them
Then after this the gods received again their daily offerings
Though their numbers were no less, but became even greater
While the racket, their clamor and clatter, grew ever louder!

TABLET II

Six-hundred years, not even six-hundred years went by
The inhabited land sprawled and the people grew plentiful
And the inhabited lands raised a howl like a bellowing bull
But the god was annoyed by all the noise that they made
Ellil had to put up with all of their loud clamor and clatter
Ellil raised his voice to be heard, speaking to the high gods,
"The noise which is made by man has become too great,
All of this clamor and clatter has kept me from my sleep
Now let us make it so the humans will be denied their food!
So that growth will not be great enough to cure their hunger!
Let it be so, that in the heavens Adad will withhold his rain,
And beneath no subterranean water will gush from springs
Cause the winds to be unleashed and rage, denuding the soil
Let there be clouds aloft in the sky, but which bring no rain
So the farmers' fields will yield hardly any crop to speak of
Let Nissaba hold back the nourishing flow from her breasts
There are to be no blessings which are bestowed unto them
So that their **lives will be wretched and** filled with misery.'"
**[Then the gods sent messengers to Adad to withhold his rain,
To Nissaba to withhold the nourishing flow of her breasts,
And the winds were unleashed and raged, denuding the soil
There were clouds aloft in the sky, but they brought no rain
So the farmer's fields yielded hardly any crop to speak of**

There were no blessings which were bestowed unto them
So that their lives became wretched and filled with misery
Atrahasis raised his voice to be heard, speaking to his lord,
"How long are we going to be beset by this terrible famine?
Is it their intention that we bear this syndrome for all time?"
Enki raised his voice to be heard, speaking to his servant,
"Bring together the elders, gather to you the men of rank!
So as to instigate a rebellion within your own community
Send out messengers to announce this within every district
And cause them to raise a loud cry throughout all lands,
That you no longer will pay fitting homage to your gods
That you no longer beseech the favor of your goddesses
But rather find your way to the door of the rain god Adad
Present him a loaf of baked bread, leave a flour offering,
And let him feel his own shame upon receiving these gifts
So that he might remove from you his discredited hand."
Atrahasis did as he was told, bringing the elders to his door
And he raised his voice to be heard, speaking to the elders,]
"I have brought together the elders, and the men of rank,
So as to instigate a rebellion within our own community
Send out messengers to announce this within every district
And cause them to raise a loud cry throughout all lands
That you no longer will pay fitting homage to your gods
That you no longer beseech the favor of your goddesses
But rather find your way to the door of the rain god Adad

Atrahasis

Present him a loaf of baked bread, leave a flour offering,
And let him feel his own shame upon receiving these gifts
That he might remove from off of us his discredited hand
To condense a misty haze that will appear in the morning,
So during the night he will go and beckon droplets of dew,
As patron, to restore the fruitfulness of the land nine-fold."
Thus they erected a temple in the city dedicated to Adad,
Sent out messengers to announce this within every district
And caused them to raise a loud cry throughout all lands,
So they no longer would pay fitting homage to their gods
So they no longer beseeched the favor of their goddesses
But rather made their way to the door of the rain god Adad
Presented him a loaf of baked bread, left a flour offering,
Such that he himself felt shame upon receiving these gifts
So that he removed from off of them his discredited hand
And condensed a misty haze that appeared in the morning,
So during the night he went and beckoned droplets of dew
As patron, he restored the fruitfulness of the land nine-fold,
So that the days of dryness passed, and the drought ended
Then after this the gods received again their daily offerings

But in less than three periods of time, then it came to pass,
The inhabited land sprawled and the people grew plentiful
And the inhabited lands raised a howl like a bellowing bull
So the gods were bothered by all the noise that they made

Ellil raised his voice to be heard, speaking to the high gods,

"The noise which is made by man has become too great,

All of this clamor and clatter has kept me from my sleep

Let it be that Anu and Adad shut the sky above their lands

Let it be that Sin and Nergal seal shut the middle region

And regarding the barrier which defines the limits of Ocean

It will be for Ea and his *lahmu*-men to assure it's kept closed

So Anu and Adad went and shut the sky above their lands

Sin and Nergal assured that a seal secured the middle region

And regarding the barrier which defines the limits of Ocean,

Ea and his *lahmu*-men assured that this too was kept closed

And that man of great wisdom, Atrahasis, cried every day

He would walk the riverside grass with an incense-offering

Even though there was not a murmur from the canal waters

Still, at midnight he dutifully made the sacrificial offering

And even as the lassitude of sleep was getting hold of him,

Still he spoke to the irrigation waters in the canal channels,

"May the irrigation waters carry it away, the river convey it,

Let this gift offering find its way to the feet of my lord, Ea

So that when Ea looks upon it that he will not forsake me!

So that when I sleep I might experience a portentous dream."

After this, and he'd conveyed his package upon the waters,

He sat down with his face to the river and began to weep,

And the man cried as he remained by the side of the river

There he wept while looking over the surface of the waters,

As his entreaty was making its way down into deep Apsu
And Ea heard what he had spoken, and having heeded him,
He called together his *lahmu*-men, addressing them thusly,
"Go and seek out the man who **has sent this bequest to me**
And when you find him, learn what plight has befallen him
Have him tell you everything which goes on in their lands."
So they journeyed across the magnificently broad oceans
Until they went the entire way to the Apsu water's shore
Conveying to Atrahasis the message they brought from Ea,
"Are you the weeping man who sent his plea into the Apsu?
Know that Ea has heard you and that we were sent by him."
And Atrahasis raised his voice, speaking to the *lahmu*-men,
"If it is true that Ea has heard me, then what did he receive?"
The *lahmu*-men raised their voices, speaking to Atrahasis,
"We know that even as you were being overcome by sleep,
The irrigation waters carried your gift, the river conveyed it,
And your offering found its way to the feet of your lord, Ea
So when Ea looked upon it he remembered you and sent us."
He lowered himself to the ground and kissed it before them
Then the *lahmu*-men went back across the waters of Ocean
Ea raised his voice to be heard, speaking to his officer Usmu,
"Go forth and seek out Atrahasis, and convey my decision:
That the state of your lands arises from the people's actions."
And thus Usmu, Ea's officer, raised his voice to Atrahasis,
"The state of your lands is the result of the people's actions

If there is no water to speak of and **fields** engender no longer,
This has come about because there is very little that I can do
If the gods have abandoned you this is why you are forsaken
The land is like a youth who has fallen down upon his face
And having fallen no longer gets succor from the sky's teats
The land has fallen like a fig which is lying upon the ground
The teats of heaven are closed up and are not given to stream
The waters of the Abyss below are dammed and will not flow
Thus from this have the dark plowed lands become blanched
From this the pastures lie fallow, unadorned by rising grain."
So from on high, no rain descended to fill the canal works
Below, subterranean waters no longer gushed from springs,
There was no delivery which sprung from the earth's womb
Nothing green took root **and no plants grew into fruition**
The folks no longer gazed **over the bands of growing wheat**
The black soil of the countryside had been blanched white
The landscape everywhere lay encrusted with a salty dust
For the first year they consumed any grain that was in store
For the next there was none left to take from the storerooms
In the third year they were showing the signs of starvation
So that their faces were a matrix of sores, like malted grain,
And they remained alive only by **clinging urgently onto** life
Their faces became sunken; they walked bent-over in public
Their shoulders, once steadfastly set, were now slouching
Their former bearing, once raised aloft, was now drooping

So they conveyed the message from Atrahasis to the gods
Setting the matter forth before the gathering of the high gods,
They convened, **prepared to address the situation facing them**
The words which had been sent by Atrahasis were conveyed
Setting the matter forth before **the gathering of the high gods,**
["How long are we going to be beset by this terrible distress?
Is it their intention that we bear this syndrome for all time?"
Then Ellil raised his voice, speaking to his children the gods,
"No longer shall the diseases be unleashed upon mankind,
Though their numbers are no less, but are even greater still!
Though I am just as annoyed by the racket that they make,
And am yet unable to sleep from all their clamor and clatter!
Then let us make it so the humans will be denied their food!
Make it so that there is not enough corn to fill their stomachs!
And make it so that Adad in heaven will hold back his rains,
Beneath will he act to assure waters do not gush from springs!
So that the farmer's fields no longer produce in abundance
Let Nissaba hold back the nourishing flow from her breasts
So the black soil of the countryside becomes blanched white
So the landscape everywhere is encrusted with a salty dust
Let earth deny her succor, so nothing grows, not even grain
Make it so that people are plagued by the horrible disease,
Constrict the birth channel so as to deny a prosperous birth!"
Thus they made it so the humans would be denied their food
Making it so there was not enough corn to fill their stomachs

Made it so that Adad in heaven would hold back his rains,
Beneath he acted to assure waters did not gush from springs
So that the farmer's fields no longer produced in abundance
And Nissaba held back the nourishing flow from her breasts,
So the black soil of the countryside became blanched white
So the landscape everywhere lay encrusted with a salty dust
And earth denied her succor, so nothing grew, not even grain,
Made it so the people were plagued by the horrible disease,
Constricting the birth canal so as to deny a prosperous birth
Ea with his *lahmu*-men were watchful at the bolt of the sea
On high, Adad made it so that his rains were in short supply
Below, subterranean waters no longer gushed from springs
So that the farmer's fields no longer produced in abundance
And Nissaba held back the nourishing flow from her breasts]

Six-hundred years, not even six-hundred years went by
The inhabited land sprawled and the people grew plentiful,
(And the inhabited lands raised a howl like a bellowing bull)
But the god was annoyed by all the noise that they made
And could get no sleep with all of their incessant clamor
Ellil convened a congress, speaking to his children the gods,
"The noise which is made by man has become too great,
So that I have become agitated from their eternal racket,
And I am denied sleep from all of their incessant clamor
We'll have Namtar put an end to this din without delay!

And bring on malaise, the shivering, and horrible diseases
To be unleashed in a fury, with the violence of a hurricane."
So the order was given, the shivering disease was unleashed
And they had Namtar put a stop to their din without delay
Malaise, shivering, and horrible diseases came like a storm
But the upright man Atrahasis heard the word of his lord Ea
Atrahasis raised his voice to be heard, speaking to his god,
And in answer he heard the word spoken by **his master** Ea
Atrahasis raised his voice to be heard, speaking to his god,
"My master, the people are overcome with groans of agony!
The disease outbreak of the gods is obliterating the country!
Master Ea, the people are overcome with groans of agony!
The disease outbreak of the gods is obliterating the country!
As you made man, you should put an end to these maladies,
Bring an end to the diseases: malaise, shivering, and horrible
Then Ea raised his voice to be heard, speaking to Atrahasis,
"Bring together the elders, gather to you the men of rank!
Send out messengers to announce this within every district
And cause them to raise a loud cry throughout all lands
That you no longer will pay fitting homage to your gods
That you no longer beseech the favor of your goddesses
[Discontinue the performance of the holy rites of Namtar!
Present him a loaf of baked bread, leave a flour offering,
Find your way to the door of Namtar and beseech to him,
That by these offerings he will remove his discredited hand."]

Tablet II

Ellil convened a congress, speaking to his children the gods,
"No longer shall the diseases be unleashed upon mankind,
Though their numbers are no less, but are even greater still!
Though I am just as annoyed by the racket that they make,
And am yet unable to sleep from all their clamor and clatter!
Thus let us make it so the humans will be denied their food!
Make it so that there is not enough corn to fill their stomachs!
And make it so that Adad in heaven will hold back his rains,
Beneath will he act to assure waters do not gush from springs!
So that the farmer's fields no longer produce in abundance
Let Nissaba hold back the nourishing flow from her breasts
So the black soil of the countryside becomes blanched white
So the landscape everywhere is encrusted with a salty dust
Let earth deny her succor, so nothing grows, not even grain
Make it so that people are plagued by the horrible disease,
Constrict the birth channel so as to deny a prosperous birth!"
Thus they made it so the humans would be denied their food
Making it so there was not enough corn to fill their stomachs
Made it so that Adad in heaven would hold back his rains,
Beneath he acted to assure waters did not gush from springs
So that the farmer's fields no longer produced in abundance
And Nissaba held back the nourishing flow from her breasts,
So the black soil of the countryside became blanched white
So the landscape everywhere lay encrusted with a salty dust
And earth denied her succor, so nothing grew, not even grain

Atrahasis

Made it so the people were plagued by the horrible disease,
Constricting the birth canal so as to deny a prosperous birth
Ea with his *lahmu*-men were watchful at the bolt of the sea
On high, Adad made it so that his rains were in short supply
Below, subterranean waters no longer gushed from springs
So that the farmer's fields no longer produced in abundance
And Nissaba held back the nourishing flow from her breasts,
So the black soil of the countryside became blanched white
So the landscape everywhere lay encrusted with a salty dust
And earth denied her succor, so nothing grew, not even grain
Made it so the people were plagued by the horrible disease,
Constricting the birth canal so as to deny a prosperous birth
Thereby the lands were beset by famine, its people by misery
[For the first year they consumed any grain that was in store]
For the next there was none left to take from the storerooms
In the third year they were showing the signs of starvation
By the fourth year their once steadfast shoulders slouched
Unlike previous years, they now walked bent-over in public
And these were the circumstances when the fifth year came:
The daughter looked with contempt on her mother's arrival
And the mother would fail to invite her own daughter inside
The daughter kept her eye on the scales at her mother's sale
The mother kept her eye on the scales at her daughter's sale
By the time the sixth year came, the daughter was the meal
And the honorable son was distinguished as the main course

Thus were all the generations of mankind consumed by Fate
Until there were only but one or two homes still left occupied
So that their faces were a matrix of sores, like malted grain,
And they remained alive only by **clinging urgently onto** life
But the upright man Atrahasis, heard the word of his lord Ea
Atrahasis raised his voice to be heard, speaking to his god,
He removed himself from his god's communication conduit
Instead he set his bed nearby to the canals, which spoke not
[Still, at midnight he dutifully made the sacrificial offering
And even as the lassitude of sleep was getting hold of him,
Still he spoke to the irrigation waters in the canal channels,
"May the irrigation waters carry it away, the river convey it,
Let this gift offering find its way to the feet of my lord, Ea
So that when Ea looks upon it that he will not forsake me!
So that when I sleep I might experience a portentous dream."
And Ea heard what he had spoken, and having heeded him,
He called together his *lahmu*-men, addressing them thusly,
"Go and seek out the man who has sent this bequest to me."
So they journeyed across the magnificently broad oceans
Until they went the entire way to the Apsu water's shore
Conveying to Atrahasis the message they brought from Ea
He lowered himself to the ground and kissed it before them
Then the *lahmu*-men went back across the waters of Ocean
Ea raised his voice to be heard, speaking to his officer Usmu,
"Go forth and seek out Atrahasis, and convey my decision,

That the state of your lands comes from the people's actions."

And from on high, no rain descended to fill the canal works
Below, subterranean waters no longer gushed from springs
There was no delivery which sprung from the earth's womb
Nothing green took root and no plants grew into fruition
The folks no longer gazed over the bands of growing wheat
The black soil of the countryside had been blanched white
The landscape everywhere lay encrusted with a salty dust
For the first year they consumed any grain that was in store]
For the next there was none left to take from the storerooms
In the third year they were showing the signs of starvation
By the fourth year their once steadfast shoulders slouched
Unlike previous years, they now walked bent-over in public
And these were the circumstances when the fifth year came:
The daughter looked with contempt on her mother's arrival
And the mother would fail to invite her own daughter inside
The daughter kept her eye on the scales at her mother's sale
The mother kept her eye on the scales at her daughter's sale
By the time the sixth year came, the daughter was the meal
And the honorable son was distinguished as the main course
Thus were all the generations of mankind consumed by Fate
Until there were only but one or two homes still left occupied
So that their faces were a matrix of sores, like malted grain,
And they remained alive only by **clinging urgently onto** life

So they conveyed the message from Atrahasis to the gods
They convened, **prepared to address the situation facing them**
The words which had been sent by Atrahasis were conveyed
"How long [**are we going to be beset by this terrible distress?**]
Is it their intention that we bear this syndrome for all time?"
[Then Ellil raised his voice, speaking to his children the gods,
"No longer shall the diseases be unleashed upon mankind,
Though their numbers are no less, but are even greater still!
Though I am just as annoyed by the racket that they make,
And am yet unable to sleep from all their clamor and clatter!
Thus let us make it so the humans will be denied their food!
Make it so that there is not enough corn to fill their stomachs!
And make it so that Adad in heaven will hold back his rains,
Beneath will he act to assure waters do not gush from springs!
So that the farmer's fields no longer produce in abundance
Let Nissaba hold back the nourishing flow from her breasts
So the black soil of the countryside becomes blanched white
So the landscape everywhere is encrusted with a salty dust
Let earth deny her succor, so nothing grows, not even grain
Make it so that the people are plagued by the horrible disease,
Constrict the birth channel so as to deny a prosperous birth!"
Thus they made it so the humans would be denied their food
Making it so there was not enough corn to fill their stomachs
Made it so that Adad in heaven would hold back his rains,
Beneath he acted to assure waters did not gush from springs

So that the farmer's fields no longer produced in abundance
And Nissaba held back the nourishing flow from her breasts,
So the black soil of the countryside became blanched white
So the landscape everywhere lay encrusted with a salty dust
And earth denied her succor, so nothing grew, not even grain
Made it so the people were plagued by the horrible disease,
Constricting the birth canal so as to deny a prosperous birth
Ea with his *lahmu*-men were watchful at the bolt of the sea
On high, Adad made it so that his rains were in short supply
Below, subterranean waters no longer gushed from springs
So that the farmer's fields no longer produced in abundance
And Nissaba held back the nourishing flow from her breasts]

[Ellil convened a congress, speaking to his children the gods,]
"Adad caused his rain to pour down in buckets abundantly,
So streaming water was plentiful throughout the meadowland
Clouds were so numerous that they nearly blotted out the sky
They must not feed on Nissaba's grain, the comfort of man."
The god sat beset with nerves, troubled there in the congress,
Enki sat beset with nerves, and troubled there in the congress
There was a great amount of tension between Enki and Ellil
The warrior Ellil was aware that this breach was done by Enki
And that the other gods had repealed what they had decided
And he was stomping mad from his elevated ire at the Igigi,
"Every one of us, of the great Anunna, consented to do this

The heavens were to be firmly secured by Anu and Adad,
While I was responsible for securing the earth down below,
And likewise, when Enki had arrived at his assigned place,
He was going to release the bonds and bring us liberation!
You were going to serve up an abundance unto the people!
You were supposed to take charge **and manage the scales!**"
Ellil raised his voice to be heard, saying to his officer Nusku,
"Go and gather fifty of the *lahmu*-men here **on my orders**
Go and fetch them so they are standing here in front of me."
And so fifty *lahmu*-men were brought together on his orders,
Then the chief warrior, Ellil, spoke to the *lahmu*-men, saying,
"Every one of us, of the great Anunna, consented to do this
The heavens were to be firmly secured by Anu and Adad,
While I was responsible for securing the earth down below,
And likewise, when Enki had arrived at his assigned place,
He was going to release the bonds and bring us liberation!
You were going to serve up an abundance unto the people!
You were supposed to take charge **and manage the scales!**"

But Ellil had to put up with all of the loud clamor and clatter
So Ellil, the warrior, **raised his voice to be heard, to the gods,**
"I am just as greatly annoyed by the racket that they make!
[And am yet unable to sleep from all their clamor and clatter!
Thus let us make it so the humans will be denied their food!
Make it so that there is not enough corn to fill their stomachs!

And make it so that Adad in heaven will hold back his rains,
Beneath will he act to assure waters do not gush from springs!
So that the farmer's fields no longer produce in abundance
Let Nissaba hold back the nourishing flow from her breasts
So the black soil of the countryside becomes blanched white
So the landscape everywhere is encrusted with a salty dust
Let earth deny her succor, so nothing grows, not even grain
Make it so the people are plagued by the horrible disease,
Constrict the birth channel so as to deny a prosperous birth!"
Thus they made it so the humans would be denied their food
Making it so there was not enough corn to fill their stomachs
Made it so that Adad in heaven would hold back his rains,
Beneath he acted to assure waters did not gush from springs
So that the farmer's fields no longer produced in abundance
And Nissaba held back the nourishing flow from her breasts,
So the black soil of the countryside became blanched white
So the landscape everywhere lay encrusted with a salty dust
And earth denied her succor, so nothing grew, not even grain
Made it so the people were plagued by the horrible disease,
Constricting the birth canal so as to deny a prosperous birth
Ea with his *lahmu*-men were watchful at the bolt of the sea
On high, Adad made it so that his rains were in short supply
Below, subterranean waters no longer gushed from springs
So that the farmer's fields no longer produced in abundance

Tablet II

And Nissaba held back the nourishing flow from her breasts[*]

Ellil convened a congress, speaking to his children the gods,]
"You are the ones who passed your burdens onto mankind
You are the ones who gave voice to man that he might speak
And you have slain a god altogether along with his mind
So you must do something about it and bring about a flood
You ought to utilize your power against your own people!
You have so far proceeded **wrongly**, thus do the opposite
We must give astute Enki an oath which he must swear to."
Enki raised his voice to be heard, saying to his fellow gods,
"Why on earth would you force me to swear to an oath?
Why too should I utilize my power against my own people?
And this great flood you speak of, what are you implying?
I'm confused by what you mean, is it even in my power?
Rather this sort of vandalism is something Ellil should do!
He himself should select **the manner by which this happens**
So that he will be the one who gets Adad to boom in the sky
With Shullat and Hanish walking ahead like chamberlains,
So Errakal will rip out every one of the pins from their bars,
While Nimrod will come on hard and breach every blockade[12]
The Great Ones, the Anunnaki, will be required to bear torches
That they might illuminate the country with their radiant light

---

[*] These last two segments are essentially repeated again, but left out here.

So when Adad comes all light will be swallowed into darkness
He will rear up and then go about trampling the terror-stricken
On the first day a tempest will rise, blowing in an awful fury,
Unleashing the dreaded Flood-weapon; and rage like a war
The explosive annihilation-weapon will descend over the people
Who will lose sight of one another in the sheets of pouring rain
Even the gods will be alarmed by the full force of their flood
They will retreat to the safety of the highest heaven of Anu
Where they will cower like dogs, kneeling by an outlying wall
There they will stay, brought to their knees, and crying tears,
Their lips will not utter and will be foaming over with spittle
Wind will rage six days and seven nights, the tempest prevail
And every man and woman will have been reduced to clay."
[Then Ellil raised his voice, speaking to his children the gods,]
"The words you heard Enki speak are of no significance to us,
You know the land is full, and how much they have multiplied
And how we have been so annoyed by all the noise they make
So that we cannot get any sleep from all their incessant clamor
[You are the ones who passed your burdens onto mankind
You are the ones who gave voice to man that he might speak
And you have slain a god altogether along with his mind
So you must do something about it and bring about a flood
You ought to utilize your power against your own people!
You have so far proceeded wrongly, thus do the opposite."
And the congress decided in favor of the flood Ellil desired

Enki raised his voice to be heard, speaking to the high gods,]
"This divine assembly **has agreed to do something unfounded**
You should not have listened **to the justifications put forward**
But you have made your commands strict and irrevocable,
And Ellil has achieved something horrendous for the people!"

TABLET III

Atrahasis raised his voice to be heard, speaking to his master,[13]
When he was at the reed hut where he spoke to his lord Enki,
"I have experienced a portentous dream, which was terrible,
The waters of the river began to surge, turning up and rising,
Flooding its banks, and spreading over the entire landscape
There I struggled for breath, as though all life was ending
But as to what it might have meant, this was not made clear
It would be best if it was made known to me while dreaming.
So the meaning of a dream received as an omen is certain."
Enki raised his voice to be heard, speaking to his servant,
"I sent the dream to relate to you what you need to know."
Atrahasis raised his voice to be heard, speaking to his master,
"Lord, please make known to me the meaning of my dream
Tell me plainly that I might understand its implications."
Enki raised his voice to be heard, speaking to his servant,
"You say, 'It should be made known to me while dreaming'
So pay heed to the substance that I will pass along to you.
Wall, hear every utterance! Reed hut, attend to every word!
Take apart your house and with the timbers construct a boat
Put aside your property for the sake of saving living things
The boat you construct must be sized with proper proportion[14]
The length of it and the width of it should be equivalent
Put a roof upon it, like that which covers the deep Apsu,

96

Cover it all so that even the sun might not peek inside!

Construct within it both upper decks and lower decks

The ropes must be made durable enough to endure strain,

The bitumen must be made strong, to lend it sturdiness

For I will make the rains fall upon you where you stand,

Descending like a wealth of fowl, like a treasure of fish."

Atrahasis opened up the sand timer to fill it with sand,

Enki told him the amount of sand that would be required

Enough to last the duration of the flood, for seven nights

Atrahasis heard every word that Enki had spoken to him

He brought together the elders, who assembled at his door

Atrahasis raised his voice to them that he might be heard,

"My lord Enki is not popular right now with your lord Ellil

The two gods are in the midst of a feud with one another

Thus they have caused me to be driven from my house

But because I have always treated Enki with devotion,

He spoke concerning this trial which I am to undergo

No longer will I be able to remain within **your city walls**

Never again might I set my feet upon Ellil's dear land

But down into the Apsu must I travel, to be with Enki

This is what he spoke to me and this is what I must do.[15]

If I do this then he will make it rain abundantly for you,

He will send down a wealth of fowl and a treasure of fish

He will shower a downpour in prosperity, a cornucopia

In the morning it will spread over you like thick syrup

In the evening you will drown in an abundance of heaps."

Thus when the first sign of dawn appeared the next day
The elders assembled together the entire people there
The carpenter with his axe, the reed worker with his stone
The young children came with the stocks of bitumen
The poor folks fetched everything else that was required
On the fifth day he was able to lay out the frame's form
It spanned over the area of an acre, with walls ten poles high
Then he designed its form, drew out the plan for her decks
To feed the workmen every week he slaughtered an ox
To feed them every day he slaughtered a fine fat sheep
Giving them ale and beer as if there were no tomorrow
Pouring out oil and wine to the workers as if it were water
Every day was like the feast at the New Year's Day festival
When the sun appeared on the final day he gave them balm
By the time the sun had set that day the boat was complete
Everything that inhabited the meadows he had brought in,
Everything that inhabited the wild spaces he brought in:
Pure ones and impure ones, and tall ones and short ones
Fat ones and skinny ones, and large ones and small ones
He chose from among these and put them aboard the boat
Birds that are in the skies, the moaning cattle of Shakkan
The savage beasts that roam throughout the wild expanses
He chose from among these and put them aboard the boat

And he took with him every manner of skilled craftsman

He then brought all of his people **together within his barn**
Inviting them to join him before disembarking, to feast
They were seated when he sneaked his family on board
While they were all eating and while they were drinking
He did not keep still, but kept going out and coming back in,
He was crushed, his heart was breaking, he was vomiting
Then the cast of the sky altered and the clouds rumbled
When he heard that sound he closed up the door with pitch
During that entire span, as he was sealing around the door,
He could hear the storm god booming within the clouds
The winds whipped around the ship, even as he climbed up,
When he cut through the mooring rope and freed his boat
The next day there came lowering gray clouds over the sky,
An ominous gloom arose and approached like a tempest,
And an unnatural darkness prevailed over the landscape
This brought the Anzu-bird forth, flapping and screeching
Overhead the sky resounded; all of the people gazed aloft
Anzu was scratching at heaven with his fearsome claws
Lightning blazed the sky and earthquakes struck the land
He broke **through the firmament and formed a gaping hole**
From this hole in the firmament the torrent's fury poured
The Flood-weapon was unleashed upon the people like a war
They lost sight of one another within the cascading rain

Atrahasis

The storm surge roared like a charging, bellowing bull
The wind sounded like a howling ass in the wilderness
Thick dark enveloped the entire earth, the sun was not seen
The people became like a white-sheep **offering to the gods**
Every one of them was consumed by the turbulent purge
Even the gods were alarmed by the full force of the flood
They retreated to the safety of the highest heaven of Anu
Where they cowered like dogs from the crash of the deluge
The flood surge wreaked havoc, was raging out of control,
Anu lost his mind; **the gods,** his sons, **shook** around him
The lips of the great mother goddess, Nintu, were salty
All the gods, the Anunna, were left hungry and thirsty
But the divine midwife, wise Mami,[*] gazed out and cried,
"Bring sunlight back to them **so that they might see!**
How could I, within the very assembly of the gods,
How could I ever have consented to their destruction?
Ellil had a callous enough nature to command this evil
He should have withdrawn that command, like Tiruru
They lash out with anguished curses directed at me
Now they have become like white lambs of sacrifice,
Beyond my control, for how could I live with this loss?
My busy din upon earth has been reduced to silence
What must I do, must I hide myself beyond the sky?

---

[*] The mother goddess, Nintu

To live evermore in a cloister, cut off from my kith,
With what reason then did Anu accept this decision?
It came about from the command to his obedient sons
He didn't deliberate the matter, he just ordered a flood
And brought the people to a sad and sorry destruction
He conspired to bring about their pitiless decimation
Now their shining faces will never again see the light."
The gods cowered like dogs from the crash of the deluge
The flood surge wreaked havoc, was raging out of control,
Anu lost his mind; the gods, his sons, shook around him
Nintu was screaming **and wailing like a woman in travail**
"Would a genuine father have unleashed the **wild waters**
To meet their end clogging up the river like dragonflies?
Their bodies wash upon the banks like overturned boats
They bobble like a raft abandoned in the wilderness
I have seen them there, I have wept over their corpses!
Will there be an end to the tears that I shed for them?"
Nintu wailed and expressed her feelings of grief fully
The gods joined her in weeping for the vanished country
She was overcome with heartache, but could find no beer
The same spot where she wept, so the great gods did too
Managing in their speech only the sound of bleating sheep
Parched with thirst, from their lips came only emptiness
For the duration of seven entire days and seven nights
Whirling water, the storm wind, and the flood prevailed[16]

When the next day arrived the tempest, flood, and fury,
Which had been thrashing like a mother straining in birth,
All suddenly expired, and the swirling sea became still,
The storm wind lessened, the raging torrent refrained
Atrahasis peeped out a gap to see what things were like,
All quiet, nowhere distinguishable a man from the mud
There was just the endless flood water, like a flat roof
He opened the window and light beamed onto his face
He knelt down and sat, then cried with tears cascading
He looked for the hills and for the banks of the ocean
Then he saw areas of land breaking the surface of water
The boat settled itself upon the mountain of Nimush
It took hold of the craft and would not let it wander
For the first and second day, for the third and fourth day
For the fifth and sixth day, the boat did not move an inch
Then upon the seventh day Atrahasis released a dove—
It flew out and came back, finding no place to perch,
Then he reached his hand forth and released a swallow—
The swallow flew here and there, then came back home
For there was no promising place it might alight upon
Then he reached his hand forth and released a raven—
The raven flew, and seeing that the waters were receding
It settled to eat, preen, fluff itself, and did not return
He sent out everything in all directions, and sacrificed
Setting down the ritual offering on the mountain peak

Setting out the jars **in seven columns and in seven rows**

And into them he poured the oils of reed, pine, and myrtle

The gods smelled the rising smoke, a pleasing fragrance

They gathered over the offering like a swarm of flies

After they consumed the offering, Nintu rose and spoke,

"What could have come over Anu to make this decision?

And does Ellil have no shame coming to savor the smoke?

Without consideration the two of them sent down a flood

And brought the people to a sad and sorry destruction

They agreed to cause their dire and pitiless obliteration

Now their shining faces will never again look on the sun."

She approached the great flies which Anu had fashioned

"From now on man's burden will be a burden which I share

From now his fate will no longer be separated from my own

He must now save me from any harm, by offering sacrifice

And so let me rise every day in the morning **for his sake**

Recognize, O gods, that I will never forget this calamity!

May these big flies become *lapis lazuli* upon my necklace

I will eternally recall and never forget what happened here."

Then Ellil, the warrior, caught his first sight of the cargo boat,

And he was stomping mad from his elevated ire at the Igigi,

"Every one of us, of the great Anunna, swore to carry this out

We agreed there was not to be one thing left alive on earth,

So how is it that any man was able to survive this disaster?"

Anu raised his voice to be heard, speaking to the warrior Ellil,
"There are none among the gods but Enki who would do so?
He made it so the reed-hut betrayed our plans beforehand."
Enki raised his voice to be heard, speaking to the high gods,
"Yes, it was I who did it, and thus did it against your wishes!
Since I worked to guarantee life was saved, not extinguished
I had this man construct the boat, and take others with him,
To save all manner of life on earth, and to return them safely
The one who does wrong is blameworthy for his own wrongs
And he who commits a crime is culpable for his own crimes
Thus I am not opposed to the exacting of any punishments,
Rather if any man acts contrarily to your commandments,
Then, by all means, exact due punishment of the offender,
Or against anyone else who contravenes your holy statutes
If you have cause for complaint, then make your case justly
Exact your punishments with equanimity, and without ire
That a man may not suffer when not guilty of wrongdoing
Rather have his numbers be reduced by the lion and wolf
Rather have his numbers be reduced by famine and plague
Rather have his numbers be reduced by war and invasion
Only that you not bring destruction to every one of them
Only that they might never suffer extinction from a flood
Thus the gods will not be known for their maliciousness
Then man will continue to make his offerings to the gods
Yet if he continues to act against to your will, then so be it,

And bring punishments to the ones who sin against you

But only exacting punishment where punishment is due

There, I have now said everything that I wished to convey!"

And Ellil raised his voice to be heard, speaking to wise Enki,

"Then let us go, and bring the womb-goddess Nintu to us!

And we will hold a conference together at the meeting hall."

Enki raised his voice to be heard, to the womb-goddess Nintu,

"Nintu, as womb-goddess you are the one who chooses fates,

You are the one who determines destinies for all the people

Have it be that a third of all people are able to have children,

Which will assure the continuance of the population of man

Have a third of them be unable to do so, due to youth or age,

Have there be a third of the people who have among them

Women who are capable of giving birth, but not properly,

May the *pasittu*-demon lift the baby from its mother's arms,

And further make the *ugbabtu*, *entu*, and *egisitu*-women:

Who are off-limits to men, to further reduce the birthrate'[7]*

Let his fortunes rise and fall, and his fate be unknown to him

Let there be among mankind but few who are prosperous,

But let the remainder of them struggle daily for survival

Sometimes mankind will be reduced from facing famine,

Sometimes mankind will be reduced from facing disease,

---

* Classes of women whose holy association made them off-limits to childbirth.

Sometimes mankind will be reduced from facing warfare,
And through these means his numbers will not burgeon
Through these means man will not become too powerful
Let it be that humankind not be allowed to live eternally
But only for a duration of time, a fixed number of years
This will be made the manner of life for all of humankind
Let there be no fixed duration for death, but only for life
And thus there will not be so many humans upon earth
There must only be enough to perform the work of gods
Let him live his life in joy and misery for his brief lifespan
May he forever enjoy only what is meant for man to enjoy
Therefore let him have a full stomach, live in mirth daily,
Plan delights for himself, celebrating both night and day
Dress in fine clothing, bathe himself, and remain unsoiled
Let him be pleased by the product of his accomplishments
Let him be honored by the excellent quality of his children
Let him be content with the company of a well-bred wife
And let him find comfort from his work in his latter years
Before he reaches his endless rest when life reaches its end
These alone are the things a mortal man might strive for
May he live a life filled with righteousness, like Atrahasis
To serve the gods, honor his parents, and aid his people
Showing due regard for both equanimity and faithfulness
Such are the things which must determine his business
Thus set down for him the instructions for him to live by

Such that man might recognizes the origin of his miseries,

And that man will be inclined to hold himself from evil,

With due regard for the gods through righteous conduct,

Never failing in making his regular offerings to the gods,

Performed at the requisite times, to incline away our wrath

Thus have them be recorded for all time to bear witness,

So that it be written for future generations to understand

Under what circumstances we brought on the Great Flood,

While a man among them was able to survive this disaster

You are the gods' advisor; I obeyed you in making discord

So have the Igigi give ear to his song, meant to honor you,

That there might always be a testimony to your greatness

So I will chant the account of the Flood to everyone, Hear!"

Bibliography

Barnstone, Willis, ed. The Other Bible. San Francisco: Harper, 1984.

Charlesworth, James H., ed. The Old Testament Pseudepigrapha. Volume 2. 1983. Peabody, Mass: Hendrickson, 2009.

Dalley, Stephanie, trans. Myths from Mesopotamia. 1989. New York: Oxford, 2000.

George, Andrew, trans. The Epic of Gilgamesh. 1999, London: Penguin, 2003.

Romer, John. Testament: The Bible and History. 1988. New York: Henry Holt, 1993.

Shinan, Avigdor and Yair Zakovitch. From Gods to God: How the Bible Debunked, Suppressed, or Changed Ancient Myths and Legends. Trans. Valerie Zakovitch. Lincoln: University of Nebraska, 2012.

Stephany, Timothy J. Blood & Incest: The Unholy Beginning of the Universe. printed by Createspace, 2014.

Stephany, Timothy J. Roar of the Tempests: A Dialogue. printed by Createspace, 2014.

Stephany, Timothy J. The Eden Enigma: A Dialogue. printed by Createspace, 2014.

Stephany, Timothy J. The Gilgamesh Cycle. printed by Createspace, 2014.

Stephany, Timothy J. The Holy Bible Revealed, Volume 2: Compositional History. printed by Createspace, 2014.

White, Gavin. Babylonian Star-Lore. London: Solaria, 2008.

Endnotes

[1] Shinan (2012), p. 10.

[2] Romer (1988), pp. 35-37.

[3] Dalley (2000), p. 7.

[4] Romer (1988), p. 32.

[5] Dalley (2000), p. 6.

[6] Dalley (2000), p. 2.

[7] Dalley (2000), p. 6.

[8] About 15 missing lines follow, consult footnote

[9] There follows an unrecoverable gap of about 25 lines, consult footnote.

[10] There follows an unrecoverable gap of about 15 lines.

[11] There follows a partly recoverable gap of about 45 lines.

[12] There follows a gap of 35 lines, partly recoverable from the 'Gilgamesh Cycle', Tablet XI.

[13] There is here a gap of about 10 lines.

[14] Many of the missing segments in the flood story are taken from the 'Gilgamesh Cycle' Tablet XI.

[15] There follows a gap of about 15 lines.

[16] There follows a significant gap of about 60 lines, partly recoverable from the 'Gilgamesh Cycle', Tablet XI.

[17] There follows a gap of about 35 lines, but their meaning is clear and is recoverable in sentiment from the 'Gilgamesh Cycle'.

CPSIA information can be obtained
at www.ICGtesting.com
Printed in the USA
LVHW052249290123
738188LV00002B/293